CULTURE SMART!

PAKISTAN

Safia Haleem

·K·U·P·E·R·A·R·D·

ISBN 978 1 85733 677 1
This book is also available as an e-book: eISBN 978 1 85733678 8

British Library Cataloguing in Publication Data
A CIP catalogue entry for this book is available from the British Library

First published in Great Britain
by Kuperard, an imprint of Bravo Ltd
59 Hutton Grove, London N12 8DS
Tel: +44 (0) 20 8446 2440   Fax: +44 (0) 20 8446 2441
www.culturesmart.co.uk
Inquiries: sales@kuperard.co.uk

Distributed in the United States and Canada
by Random House Distribution Services
1745 Broadway, New York, NY 10019
Tel: +1 (212) 572-2844   Fax: +1 (212) 572-4961
Inquiries: csorders@randomhouse.com

Series Editor Geoffrey Chesler
Design Bobby Birchall

Printed in Malaysia

About the Author

SAFIA HALEEM was born and grew up in Peshawar, northwestern Pakistan, and graduated from Peshawar University with an M.A. in English Literature. She worked as a teacher trainer in all the main cities of Pakistan before winning a British Council scholarship to study in Scotland. After gaining a postgraduate degree in Linguistics from the University of Edinburgh, she returned to Pakistan and coauthored the book *Visuals for the Language Classroom*. In 1987 she moved to London and joined the BBC. Her work as a journalist has taken her to India, Iran, China, Afghanistan, and all over Pakistan. In 2004, she was project director for the BBC World Service Trust in Afghanistan. Safia is an established writer in Pashto, her first language, and has published several novels and short stories in the language. She is also developing educational material for the Afghan Medical Association, whose voluntary work benefits people on both sides of the Afghan–Pakistan border.

**The Culture Smart! series is continuing to expand.
For further information and latest titles visit
www.culturesmart.co.uk**

contents

Map of Pakistan   7
Introduction   8
Key Facts   10

Chapter 1: LAND AND PEOPLE   12
• A Nation of Nations   12
• Geography   14
• Climate   16
• People   17
• A Brief History   17
• Boundaries and Conflict   26
• Politics   28
• Government   33
• The Economy   34

Chapter 2: VALUES AND ATTITUDES   36
• Family Ties   38
• The Feudal System   39
• Multilayered Identities   40
• Religion   41
• Honor and Shame   47
• Hospitality and Generosity   48
• Tolerance and Prejudice   50
• Attitudes to the Outside World   50
• Attitudes to Success   51
• Work Ethic   52
• Attitudes to Time   53
• Attitudes to Education   54

Chapter 3: CUSTOMS AND TRADITIONS   56
• The Islamic Year   58
• Seasonal Festivities   60
• Literary Activities   66
• Weddings   67
• Celebrating at Home   69
• Family Visits   70

- Funerals   71
- Folklore and Superstition   73

Chapter 4: MAKING FRIENDS   78
- Friendship   78
- Making Conversation   79
- Not So Private   80
- Attitudes Toward Foreigners   81
- Invitations Home   82
- Giving and Receiving Gifts   85
- Dating   87

Chapter 5: PRIVATE AND FAMILY LIFE   88
- Housing   88
- Family Living   91
- *Rishtaydari*– Keeping up with Relatives   93
- Privacy and Taboos   94
- Growing up in Pakistan   95
- Further Education   97
- Love and Marriage   98
- *Mashvara* and *Naseehat*   99

Chapter 6: TIME OUT   100
- Eating Out   101
- Food and Drink   102
- Sports and Games   106
- Cultural Activities   108
- Shopping for Pleasure   110
- Sightseeing   112

Chapter 7: TRAVEL, HEALTH, AND SAFETY   114
- Visas   115
- Arrival   116
- Getting Around   119
- Where to Stay   126
- Health   127
- Safety   129

contents

Chapter 8: BUSINESS BRIEFING   132
- Business Culture   133
- "Through Proper Channel"   135
- Arranging a Meeting   135
- Meetings   136
- Presentations   138
- Decision Making   139
- Negotiations   139
- Contracts   142
- Disputes   144
- Corruption   144
- Foreign Businesswomen   146
- Colleagues   147
- Managing Disagreement   148

Chapter 9: COMMUNICATING   150
- Language   150
- Manners and Body Language   155
- Humor   157
- The Media   158
- Telephone and Internet   161
- Mail   162
- Conclusion   162

Appendix: Everyday Expressions;
  Urdu Words and Their Meanings   164
Further Reading   165
Index   166
Acknowledgments   168

Map of Pakistan

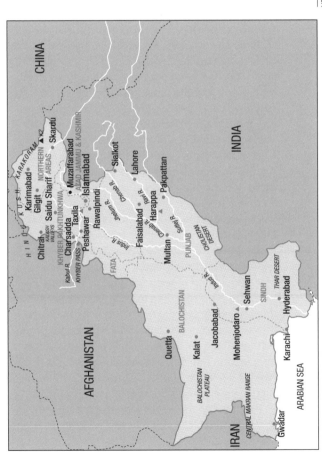

introduction

Pakistan extends along both sides of the Indus River, from its source in the snowcapped Himalayas south through green valleys, fertile plains, and arid deserts to its mouth on the Arabian Sea. The ancient Indus civilization is a reference point in the timeline of human development, and down the ages the river has sustained communities, provided communication, and given shape to the country. The historical movements of people over several centuries from Central and South Asia into Pakistan have given it a unique character, which can be seen in its rich and diverse culture, languages, literature, food, dress, and folklore. Geography gives it strategic importance, but has brought conflict to its borders and has caused much destruction through earthquakes.

Twenty-first-century Pakistan is synonymous with political turmoil, and is regarded by some as a breeding ground of terrorism and corruption. Half the country is struggling to survive a war against an unseen enemy, and the rest is coping with natural disasters, corrupt officials, and a struggle for power between the army and the feudal landlords. It has been seen in the West as a failed state, yet the people have proven to be remarkably resilient, with some significant national achievements to their credit.

Pakistan has the eighth-largest standing army in the world and is the only Muslim-majority nation to possess nuclear weapons, but very few know that it is also the land of two unique schools of art. Pakistan's national cricket team has lurched between match-fixing scandals, bitter rivalry, and shocking defeats, but its blind cricket team has won two World Cup championships. In a country where the disabled have few facilities, this is a typical Pakistani success story.

This complex nation consists of various ethnic groups, each with its own cultures and subcultures, but which are unified by the common values of hospitality, honor, and respect for elders. Strong family ties and respect for human feelings are at the core of Pakistani society. The differences in language have never been a cause of political instability. That the country has been able to hold together is mainly due to the strength of its workforce and family ties.

Pakistan has extremes of wealth and poverty. It has some of the most modern buildings and facilities, even in small towns, and is considered a shoppers' paradise by many; others call it a nation of food lovers. For most people, though, daily life is full of difficulties, yet everyone knows how to cope with crises. Creative, tough, and adaptable, Pakistanis are among the most self-reliant people in the world, bouncing back after major catastrophes.

This book takes you behind the headlines and introduces you to some of the country's little-known traditions. It describes the vitally important cultural and historical background, and shows you how Pakistanis live today. You'll discover a passionate, enterprising, and remarkable people. Strip away your preconceptions and show an interest, and you will be rewarded many times over.

Key Facts

Country Name	Islamic Republic of Pakistan	In Urdu, Islami Jamhuria Pakistan
Capital	Islamabad	Built in the 1960s specifically for government
Main Cities	Karachi, Lahore, Peshawar, Quetta, Faisalabad, Hyderabad	
Population	177,276,594 (2010 est.)	World's sixth-most populous nation
Area	Land: 300,665 sq. miles (778,720 sq. km). Water: 9,737 sq. miles (25,220 sq km)	Coastline 650 miles (1,046 km) on the Arabian Sea
Ethnic Makeup	Indo–Aryan and Mongol	
Border Countries	Afghanistan, China, India, Iran	Border disputes with India and Afghanistan
Climate	Mostly hot, dry desert, temperate in northwest, arctic in north.	Karakoram and Hindu Kush mountain ranges are snowbound for much of the year.
Government	Democratic federal republic with bicameral parliament: the Majlis-e-Shura (senate) and the Qaumi Assembly (lower house)	The president is the head of state; the prime minister is the head of government.
Administrative Areas	Balochistan, Punjab, Sindh, and Khyber Pakhtunkhwa (formerly North-West Frontier) Provinces; Islamabad; Azad Jammu and Kashmir; Gilgit-Baltistan; FATA (tribal areas)	

Literacy	Total 49%; male 63%, female 36%	Reading and writing at age 15
Languages	Punjabi 48.% Sindhi 12% Sariaki 10.% Pashto 8% Urdu 8% Balochi 3.% Hindku 2% Baruhi 1% Others 8%	English and Urdu are official national languages.
Religion	Islam 97% (Sunni 77%, Shia 20%); other (incl. Christian and Hindu) 3%	
Age Structure	0–14 years 36.9% 15–64 years 58.8% 65+ years 4.3%	
GDP	$437.5 billion (est. 2006). Real growth rate 6.6%	Per capita income $2,600; 17% below poverty line
Currency	Pakistani rupee (Rs, PKR)	
Electricity	230 volts, 50 Hz	Round-prong plugs. Frequent rolling blackouts
Video/TV	The British PAL system	
Internet Domain	.pk	
Telephone	Pakistan's country code is 92.	To call out dial 00 followed by the country code.
Time Zone	GMT + 5 hours in winter	GMT + 4 hours in summer

chapter one

LAND & PEOPLE

A NATION OF NATIONS

The name of Pakistan is heard in every news bulletin all over the world on an almost weekly basis—sadly, for all the wrong reasons. The country is described as both a victim and a culprit at the same time, yet the social and cultural reality is infinitely richer, more complex, and more nuanced than might be imagined from the news. Occupying land crisscrossed by ancient invaders, Pakistan is a young country whose history stretches back for thousands of years. It is the home of two ancient civilizations—the Indus and the Gandhara—and its culture has been shaped by invaders, nomadic tribes, clans, refugees, and preachers of various religions. It was home to some of the earliest human settlements, and the region along the eastern banks of the Indus River was a magnet to the ancient Greek and Persian empires. Numerous races came here, moved on, or settled in the fertile valleys. The flow of migration continued even in modern times, with millions entering from India at the time of Partition, from Bangladesh, and from Afghanistan at the end of the twentieth century.

"Pakistan" is a compound word, having two parts: *pak* (Persian, pure) and *stan* (Turkish, a place to live). The Muslims of India adopted the name in 1933 in their demand for a separate and independent homeland. Pakistan is in essence a multiethnic and multilingual nation that is home to people of various regional nationalities. Nation building has been a difficult process. The country has undergone a succession of traumatic sociopolitical experiences since achieving independence; but it continues to demonstrate resilience and the capacity to survive and adapt to changing circumstances.

Pakistan has a well-established infrastructure and legal system, which makes it attractive for investment. It has strong human resources, including an English-speaking workforce, cost-effective managers, and skilled technical workers. The people of Pakistan are warm and welcoming. Their great love of art can even be seen on painted trucks. Their *qawwali* music, performed in the shrines of famous Sufi saints in Punjab and Sindh, is unique, and attracts millions of people every year who come to make a wish or offer alms and to listen to the music and poetry recitals. The Pakistani passion for cricket is proverbial, and there is a team in every locality with aspiring young players who want to be on the national team. The cities of

Lahore, Karachi, Sialkot, and Faisalabad are thriving with textile and other industries and attracting new investors for business and trade.

Pakistan offers a variety of landscapes, from the seaside in Karachi, to the glacial mountains of the north, home to the second-highest peak (K2) in the world, the valleys of Swat with ski resorts, the romantic Khyber Pass, the desert of Cholistan and the fossils of Balochistan, where a skeleton of a dinosaur was discovered a few years ago. It is a principal gateway to Central Asia and has good connections with the Middle East and South Asia. There is a growing domestic market attracting both foreign investors and the Pakistani diaspora.

GEOGRAPHY

Pakistan is located between the important regions of South Asia, Central Asia, and the greater Middle East. It has a 650-mile (1,046 km) coastline along the Arabian Sea and the Gulf of Oman in the south. It is bordered by Afghanistan and Iran in the west, India in the east, and China in the far northeast. The main

river is the Indus, which flows the length of the country and is fed by the combined waters of three of the five rivers of Punjab—the Chenab, Jhelum, and Ravi. The waters of the other two rivers, the Beas and the Sutlej, which rise in the Himalayas, are largely used for irrigation in India. Along the Indus and its tributaries are found most of Pakistan's population, its chief agricultural areas, and its major hydroelectric power stations.

The border of Pakistan's northern territory runs through the mountains of the Karakorum Range, which it shares with Afghanistan and China. Five of the fourteen highest mountain peaks in the world are in Pakistan and it is home to the second-highest mountain in the world, K2, at 28,251 feet (8,611 m).

Geologically, Pakistan overlaps both the Indian and the Eurasian tectonic plates. The northern areas lie mainly in central Asia, along the edge of the Indian plate, and are prone to violent earthquakes where the two plates collide. The most devastating earthquake happened in 2005. In the northeast is the disputed territory of Kashmir, the Pakistani part of which also borders China. The Balochistan Plateau,

toward the west of the country, occupies the largest province, with an elevation between 1,000 and 3,000 feet (300–900 m) above sea level. It joins the Thar Desert and Lower Indus Valley in the south, which forms Sindh Province. The western mountains are full of natural energy resources, including gas and coal mines; the rich soil of Punjab produces the best cotton in the world.

CLIMATE

Pakistan lies in the temperate zone, immediately above the Tropic of Cancer. Arid conditions exist in the coastal south, characterized by a monsoon season with adequate rainfall, mostly in the province of Punjab. There are wide variations of extreme temperatures between north and south. The coastal area along the Arabian Sea is usually warm, whereas the frozen ridges of the Karakorum Range and of other mountains of the far north are snowcapped most of the year and accessible by world-class climbers only for a few weeks in the summer. The hottest place in the subcontinent is Jacobabad in Sindh Province, with temperatures of nearly 130°F (54°C) in the month of June. Rainfall varies from as little as less than 10 inches to over 150 inches a year in various parts of the country.

There are four seasons: a cool, dry winter marked by mild temperatures from December through February; a hot, dry spring from March through May; the summer rainy season, or southwest monsoon period, from June through September; and the mild autumn period of October and November.

PEOPLE

Pakistan has a multicultural and multiethnic society and hosts one of the largest refugee populations in the world, mainly from Afghanistan. This diversity is more visible along cultural and linguistic, rather than religious or genetic lines. Almost all Pakistanis belong to the Indo-Aryan ancestral groups that include Punjabis, Pashtuns, Sindhi, Balochi, Baruhi, Balti, and dozens of other smaller groups. In the northern mountains are some of the oldest Aryan peoples, the Dardic, Kashmiri, and Swati. Urdu-speaking migrants from India known as Muhajirs, mostly living in Karachi, are grouped on a linguistic rather than an ethnic basis.

The estimated population of Pakistan in 2011 was over 187 million, making it the world's sixth-most populous country. About 95 percent of its people are Muslim, with the remainder made up of small groups of Hindus, Christians, Sikhs, Parsis (Zoroastrians), Buddhists, and followers of other faiths. The majority of the Muslims are of the Sunni Hanafi branch, and others are Shia.

A BRIEF HISTORY

Prehistory

The oldest stone tool in the world, dating back 2.2 million years, was found at Rabat, near Islamabad. The largest hand axe found in the Soan Valley and quartz tools from a cave in Mardan date from 50,000 BCE.

The site of Mehergarh, between the cities of Quetta and Kalat in western Balochistan Province, discovered by French archaeologists in 1974, has added to our knowledge about human history in Pakistan. The earliest settlement in this small farming village dates to between 7000 BCE and 5500 BCE. Six mounds have been excavated, yielding about 32,000 artifacts, including some beautiful painted pottery. The settlement was on a travel route between Persia and India used by migrants for thousands of years and is considered more ancient than the Khyber Pass. The excavation proves that there were continuous settlements in the Indus region dating back to 7,000 BCE. There are twenty such villages exposed on the banks of the Indus, and a clear picture is emerging of the signs of human settlement in this area.

The Indus

The Indus River, sometimes known as "the Lion River" or "Abasin" ("the father of rivers"), is a lifeline for the many communities living along its banks. In the seventh millennium BCE, the Early Bronze Age culture emerged in villages of Sindh, Balochistan, Punjab, and Khyber Pakhtunkhwa Province. It is this social and cultural change that led to the rise of the famous cities of Mohenjodaro and Harappa along the banks of the mighty river. They were inhabited by the largest concentrations of population, including artisans, craftsmen, businessmen, and rulers. This culminated in the peak of the Indus civilization, which was primarily based on intensive irrigated agriculture and overseas trade and contact with Persia, the Gulf States,

Mesopotamia, and Egypt. A picture of this time is frozen at the city of Mohenjodaro, the first planned city in the world, in which streets are aligned straight and parallel, with others crossing at right angles. It was the first literate civilization of the subcontinent, which lasted for nearly five hundred years and flourished up to 1750 BCE.

The Aryans

Around 1500 BCE there was an influx of nomadic tribes from Central Asia, caused by climate change and the need to search for water. This steady stream of new people reached the banks of the rivers flowing into the Indus Valley. Known to historians as Aryans, their legacy is the body of thousands of hymns called Vedas. These hymns are celebrations of nature, and almost all the main rivers of Pakistan are mentioned in them.

The Indus civilization, based on trade and industry, saw the arrival of horse-riding pastoralists who barely understood the system of irrigated agriculture and the value of dams. The Aryans developed their own religion, practiced animal sacrifice, and gradually built up tribal kingdoms along the Indus Valley. The most prominent of these was the Gandhara, with capitals at Pushkalavati (modern Charsadda) and Taxila. The Aryan tribes are known from the large number of their graves and from their village settlements all over Swat, Dir, and Bajaur, up to Taxila, and from the rock carvings they left along the Karakorum Highway.

The Persians

The city of Taxila began to grow from around the sixth century BCE, when the Achaemenian kings

Cyrus and Darius sent expeditions to the Indus. Excavations show the use of iron technology in that period to produce tools, weapons, and other objects for daily use. Above all, a new form of writing known as Kharoshti was developed here. At the same time the world's oldest university was founded at Taxila. It was here that the future ruler of India, Chandra Gupta Maurya, who later founded the first subcontinental empire in South Asia, received his education. His grandson, Ashoka, introduced Buddhism into Gandhara and built the first Buddhist monastery at Taxila.

The Bactrian Greeks

The Persian Achaemenian Empire collapsed under the onslaught of Alexander of Macedonia in the fourth century BCE. He crossed the Indus at Swabi and came to Taxila in 326 BCE, to be welcomed by the local king, Ambhi, in his palace at Bhir mound. Alexander then moved on to the Jhelum River, fought with Raja Porus on its banks, and conquered Multan. His exhausted army refused to go beyond

the Beas River and he had to turn back to the Makran coast to head home.

He left behind in Central Asia a number of Greeks, who founded the Greco-Bactrian kingdom of Gandhara. It lasted more than five hundred years, ruled by thirteen Greek kings and queens, and its art and religion had considerable influence on the development of the region This civilization was the result of the interaction of several peoples who followed the Greeks—Scythians, Parthians, and Kushans—who came one after the other from Central Asia by various routes and integrated into the local society. It is under their patronage that Buddhism evolved here into its new Mahayana form, and this became the religion of the contemporary people in Pakistan. Under their encouragement Buddhist monks moved freely along the "Silk Road," the great transcontinental trade route, and carried their religion to central Asia, China, Korea, and Japan. Trade along the Silk Road was controlled mainly by the Kushana emperors, who built a mighty empire with Peshawar as their capital. The Kushana period, from the first to the third centures, was the golden age of Pakistan, with the Silk Road trade bringing unparalleled prosperity to the area.

The Huns

In the third century CE, waves of Hephthlites, sometimes known as Hunas, or white Huns, appeared throughout Central Asia, setting up a new system of rule based on tribal allegiance. They established themselves by the first half of the fifth century in the northwest, then pushed toward the east, causing the Gupta Empire of India to disintegrate, and made their capital at present-day Sialkot, in Punjab, under their emperor, Mihirakula. They were driven out eventually, and little is recorded about them in the historical accounts, but they created a new form of land management that has lasted until today. The tribes have fused into an agricultural society, but their brotherhoods have survived and they have given a permanent character to northern Pakistan. There are conflicting views among historians as to whether they were the ancestors of the Turks or the Pashtuns.

The Arabs

In 711 CE, the Ummayad dynasty of the Arab Caliphate sent an army led by Mohammad bin Qasim against the ruler of Sindh, Raja Dahir. This powerful Raja had captured some Arab ships and imprisoned the sailors and their families, and the Arab governor of Iraq wanted revenge. The Muslim army was repulsed in its first three attempts, but was later successful, conquering the northwestern part of the Indus Valley. The arrival of the Muslim Arabs in Sindh led to the creation of the kingdom of Mansura, near present-day Hyderabad, as part of the Caliphate, though with local autonomy to the ruler. The Arabs also swept over the land of Afghanistan, and in the tenth century Mahmud, the Turkic king of Ghazni in Afghanistan, conquered Peshawar and set up his second capital at Chota-Lahure, near Swabi, in Khyber Pakhtunkhwa Province.

The Afghans

The foundations of a Muslim state in South Asia were firmly laid when the Ghori Sultans made the Indus country their springboard for the onward conquest of India, setting the stage for the religious boundaries that would lead to the development of the modern state of Pakistan. With the influx of Muslims, Sufi saints preached the word of God and their monumental tombs attracted people from all over the country. A succession of Afghan dynasties ruled the region through 1526, when the area was conquered by Babur, founder of the Mughal Empire.

The Mughals

The Mughals controlled the region from 1526 until 1739, making Lahore their favorite city. In the middle of the eighteenth century Ahmad Shah Abdali, the founder of Afghanistan, moved his forces several times to India and gained control of Punjab. But his weak successors lost the territory to the Sikhs.

Ranjit Singh, a Sikh explorer, took control of a large portion of Punjab and fought with the Afghan rulers to control Peshawar. However, his successors could not hold on to power and Britain took over the area.

The British Raj

In the eighteenth century the Mughal Empire in India collapsed and the enormous British mercantile combine known as the East India Company began to expand its influence over the area, effectively governing it on behalf of the British Crown. During the period of British rule, the North West Frontier was administered as part of Punjab. The Indian Rebellion of 1857, also known as the Sepoy Mutiny, was the region's last major armed struggle against the British Raj (*raj*, Hindi, reign), and ironically it was crushed with the help of soldiers recruited from Punjab. After the suppression of the Rebellion, the East India Company was abolished and the administration of India was transferred to London.

British rule consisted of areas directly administered by Westminster ("British India") as well as the princely states ruled by individual rulers under the suzerainty of the British Crown. In 1876 Queen Victoria was proclaimed "Empress of India."

Independence
The Indians started a freedom movement at the end of the nineteenth century, but the Muslims feared that once the British left they would be dominated by the Hindu majority, and demanded a separate homeland. In 1906 the various anticolonial leaders established the All-India Muslim League. It rose to popularity in the late 1930s amid fears of under-representation and the neglect of Muslims in politics. Later, the great Indian Muslim leader Muhammad Ali Jinnah espoused the Two Nation Theory, and led the Muslim League to adopt the Lahore Resolution of 1940, popularly known as the Pakistan Resolution.

In early 1947 Britain announced the decision to end its rule in India. In June the nationalist leaders of British India agreed to the proposed terms of transfer of power and independence: Pakistan was carved out of the two Muslim-majority wings in the eastern and northwestern regions of British India and comprised the provinces of Balochistan, East Bengal, the North-West Frontier Province, West Punjab, and Sindh.

"You are free to go to your temples, mosques, or any other place of worship in this state of Pakistan. You may belong to any religion, caste, or creed that has nothing to do with the business of the state . . . . in due course of time Hindus will cease to be Hindus and Muslims will cease to Muslims—not in a religious sense for that is the personal faith of an individual—but in a political sense as citizens of one state. "

Muhammad Ali Jinnah, Address to the Constituent Assembly of Pakistan, Karachi August 11, 1947

The modern state of Pakistan became a reality on August 14, 1947, in the noncontiguous Muslim majority areas known as West and East Pakistan.
The controversial division of the provinces of Punjab and Bengal caused huge upheaval, and communal riots and massacres broke out across India and Pakistan. Many millions of Muslims fled to Pakistan, and millions of Hindus and Sikhs fled to India.

BOUNDARIES AND CONFLICT

Pakistan's politics and conflicts are caused by its geographical location. It has some of the world's most controversial boundaries—in Kashmir, with India, and the Durand Line, with Afghanistan. Its western borders include the Khyber Pass and the Bolan Pass, which have served as traditional migration, invasion, and trade routes from Central Asia and Iran.

Kashmir

In the weeks prior to Partition, most of the princely states of India opted to join either India or Pakistan. However the state of Junagadh in western India had a Hindu majority with a Muslim ruler who wanted to join Pakistan. India had a legal claim on this state, as it did not share a border with the Pakistani territories. The state of Hyderabad was in the same position, and subsequently became part of India.

Jammu and Kashmir, in the Himalayan Mountains, with a majority Muslim population but headed by a Hindu Raja, could not logically be a part of India. The Pakistanis assumed that Kashmir would become a part of their new country, but this area has a strategic importance for India. For two months after the partition, the ruler of Kashmir could not decide, and the Pakistani leaders were becoming impatient and losing trust. In October 1947 truckloads of tribal Pashtuns and Pakistani paramilitary forces were sent to Kashmir to scare off the Indians. It was not an open war, and no armies were deployed, but the Raja of Kashmir left in panic. The United Nations brokered a cease-fire in Kashmir in 1948, but Pakistan had secured an arc of mountains around its northern part and the western end of the Kashmir Valley, which had the only road linking this area. The area was named Azad (Independent) Kashmir by Pakistan. India held the rest, and immediately started building a new road to secure access to the disputed territory. Since then several wars have been fought between the two countries on this border.

The Durand Line

The dispute on the western border with Afghanistan is also a legacy of the colonial era and is over a hundred years old. In 1893 British India, represented by Mortimer Durand, and the Afghan Amir Abdur Rahman Khan agreed not to exert any influence beyond the frontier between Afghanistan and India. A joint British–Afghan demarcation survey took place in 1894, covering more than a thousand miles (1,640 km). This has always been disputed by the Afghan government, which claims a frontier of more than two thousand miles (2,310 km). The colonial authorities carved a new province, the North-West Frontier Province, out of the areas annexed from Afghanistan. These territories are currently part of Pakistan and include the FATA (Federally Administered Tribal Areas). They also include the towns on the western bank of the Indus. These lands had been part of the Afghan Empire from 1747 until around 1820.

In August 2007, Pakistan urged Afghanistan to recognize the Durand Line, and former Pakistani President Musharraf called for the erection of a fence there, but was met with resistance from numerous political parties within both countries. Pashtun tribes continue to cross this border without any passports and visas, and because of this situation the whole border area has become a war zone since the Soviet invasion of Afghanistan in 1979.

POLITICS

From 1947 to 1956, Pakistan was a dominion within the Commonwealth of Nations, and included the Bengali territory of East Pakistan, which was physically separated from the western part by India. This decade was marred by political unrest and instability, resulting in the frequent collapse of civilian democratic governments. From 1947 to 1958 seven prime ministers of Pakistan either resigned or were ousted.

Pakistan became a parliamentary republic in 1956, with a new constitution, but political instability paved the way for a military takeover. On October 7, 1958, the country's civilian and first president, Iskandar Mirza, in collaboration with General Muhammed Ayub Khan, abrogated the constitution and declared martial law.

East Pakistan

General Ayub Khan was the first military president, from 1958 to 1969—a period of internal instability and a second war with India in 1965. His successor, General Yahya Khan (1969–71), faced economic grievances and political dissent in East Pakistan, which led to tension and military repression. After nine months of guerrilla warfare between the Pakistani armed forces and the Indian-backed Bengali Mukti Bahini militia, Indian intervention in East Pakistan escalated into the Indo-Pakistani War of 1971, and ultimately to the secession of East Pakistan as the independent state of Bangladesh. More than seventy thousand soldiers of the Pakistani armed forces were taken prisoner by India. General Yahya Khan immediately surrendered his executive powers to Zulfikar Ali Bhutto, who became the first and, to date, only civilian Chief Martial Law Administrator of the country.

The Balochistan Conflict

Balochistan is the largest province of Pakistan, rich in minerals and natural gas, but with the poorest people. Bhutto dismissed the coalition government of this province in 1973 on the grounds of its encouragement of a secessionist movement, smuggling, and opposition to modernization. Opposition leaders were arrested and jailed, and in 1976 the Sardari (tribal chief) system was abolished. In a joint military operation against the Balochi separatists, with a total news blackout, an estimated five thousand insurgents and three thousand government troops were killed. The insurgency continued until the fall of the Bhutto government in 1977 and the subsequent release of jailed leaders of

the region. Bhutto was removed in a coup led by
General Zia-ul-Haq in 1977. The Supreme Court of
Pakistan ordered the execution of Bhutto after he
had allegedly approved the murder of a political
opponent, and he was hanged in 1979.

The Troubles of the Tribal Areas

In 1893 the Pashtun tribes living between British
India and Afghanistan were cut off from
Afghanistan by the Durand Line. This was not
intended to interfere with the property or grazing
rights of the tribes on either side. On the Pakistani
side, the FATA (Federally Administered Tribal
Areas) cover about 10,500 square miles (17,000 sq.
km), with an estimated population of between three
and four million. The British introduced a system
of indirect rule, which was more concerned with
managing the tribes than controlling them,
because the tribespeople were heavily armed and
independent minded. Pakistan subsequently
adopted the same policy, with an appointed
political agent representing the government.

However, during the civil war in Afghanistan in
the 1980s, and the *jehad* (holy war) against the forces
of the former Soviet Union, fighters moved freely in
this area. Due to Pakistan's involvement in the *jehad*
the tribal areas turned into training grounds of
fighters and weaponry. When the Taleban came to
power in Afghanistan, this area became a safe haven
for Al-Qaeda and other dissident groups from
Islamic countries with the blessing of the Pakistani
intelligence agency.

After the events of 9/11, America's war on
terrorism in Afghanistan extended to the tribal
areas. Pakistan has sent its army to the area to

control the insurgents, but has not been successful so far. The tribes, already coping with insurgents slipping freely across the borders, started showing resentment when civilians started being killed, either by drone attacks or by the Taleban.

The Struggle for Power

General Zia banned all political parties and decided to make the country an Islamic state. He amended the constitution to bestow absolute power on himself, which he enjoyed until his death in 1989 in a plane crash. In the ensuing elections the Pakistan People's Party emerged victorious and its leader, Benazir Bhutto, was sworn in as the first Muslim woman prime minister. However, real power remained with the military, and Benazir's government was dismissed by the president in 1990.

Nawaz Sharif of the Muslim League became the new prime minister after fresh elections, but in 1993 his government was also dismissed by the president. The Supreme Court overruled the president and reinstated Sharif. Finally an agreement was reached and both the president and the prime minister resigned, paving the way for further elections. Benazir Bhutto regained power and made Farooq Leghari, a member of her own party, president.

The Pakistan Muslim League generally reflects conservatism in the political spectrum of the country. It is not considered the original Muslim League, which was the founding party of the state of Pakistan. Its center of power is in Punjab Province, but it also retains considerable support in other provinces, and is the only party in the country's history to have received a two-thirds majority in parliament (in the 1997 elections). It emphasizes the role of free markets and individual achievement as the primary factors behind economic prosperity and a strong base of capitalism. The party generally opposes the labor unions, and privatized the major heavy industries.

The Pakistan People's Party since its inception has a Social Democratic stance, though its founder, Zulfikar Ali Bhutto, himself was from a feudal family of Sindh. It favored the rich farmers, middle classes, and some labor unions, rejecting far-left politics. It supported unregulated business and finance and swung to the right wing, but never adopted communism as an ideology.

Other parties with seats in parliament are the Muttahidda Qaumi Movement (MQM), the Awami National Party (ANP), and two of the main Islamic political parties, Jamiat-ul-Ulema-Islam and Jamaat-e-Islami. Their ideologies are linguistic, nationalist, or religious. Since these parties have no chance of winning an absolute majority, they enter alliances with the main parties to form a government.

The move to insulate her government from presidential intervention failed as Benazir was again dismissed in 1997 on grounds of corruption. The following elections saw the emergence of Nawaz Sharif as prime minister, but he gradually became unpopular for his autocratic way of functioning. General Pervez Musharraf overthrew him in 1999 and took over power. Under growing pressure to reintroduce democratic rule, Musharraf relinquished his army post in November 2007. Benazir Bhutto was assassinated on 27 December, 2007. The Pakistan People's Party won the elections in February 2008. Syed Yusuf Raza Gillani formed the new civilian government, and Asif Ali Zardari became president.

GOVERNMENT

Pakistan is a federal parliamentary democracy. The president is the head of state, and the government is headed by the prime minister. The president must be Muslim and at least forty-five years of age. He serves a five-year term after being elected by the Senate, the National Assembly, and the provincial assemblies. There are two houses of parliament: the Majlis-e-Shura (senate), made up of 100 members, and the 342-member Qaumi Assembly (lower house). Some parliamentary seats are reserved for women and religious minorities. The voting age is eighteen.

Pakistan's secular legal system is based on British common law, but has been altered to allow Islamic Sharia law to obtain in certain areas, such as family law. Zulfikar Ali Bhutto's 1973 constitution reserved seats for women in both houses of parliament to ensure that women would be represented. If a woman did not win enough votes to gain a general seat, she would be eligible, depending on the number of votes she had received, for a reserved seat.

THE ECONOMY

Despite being rich in natural resources—gas, precious stones, minerals, and fertile agricultural land—Pakistan is not yet a well-developed country. Due to a lack of foreign investment and to internal conflict poverty remains a big issue. It is primarily an agricultural country, with 28 percent of the land under cultivation, watered by one of the largest natural irrigation systems in the world. Only 4 percent of the land is forested.

The most important crops are cotton, wheat, rice, sugarcane, millets, legumes, oil seeds, barley, fruits, and vegetables, which together account for more than 75 percent of the value of the total crop output. About 42 percent of the population are employed in agriculture.

Textiles are the main export. Other industries include food processing, pharmaceuticals, construction materials, paper products, fertilizer, and shrimp. Although Pakistan has huge reserves of natural gas it relies on foreign oil supplies.

Wealth distribution is highly uneven, with 10 percent of the population earning 27.6 percent of the national income. Poverty has always been higher in rural areas and lower in the cities. It increased sharply in the rural areas in the 1990s, and

the gap in income between urban and rural areas became much more significant. However, despite a calamitous civil war and callous fiscal mismanagement, the number of people living in poverty fell almost by half between 1999 and 2008. This economic growth was largely driven by exports and remittances from hardworking Pakistanis employed abroad.

At the end of 2008, Pakistan's soaring inflation had come down to around 25 percent. Nevertheless, the country was forced to turn to the International Monetary Fund for a US$7.6 billion bailout. It is ironic that instead of spending money on projects to improve the lives of their citizens, successive governments and the military establishment focused their efforts on becoming a nuclear power, in competion with India. Recently, the Pakistani media has given extensive coverage to the fact that a large portion of the annual budget goes to the military establishment.

chapter two

VALUES & ATTITUDES

The people of Pakistan have been through numerous cultural and religious changes over the centuries—experiences that have made them resilient and adaptable.

The average Pakistani is curious about other people, often making assumptions about the intentions of a stranger upon first meeting, and sometimes seeming rather nosy. Generalizing and stereotyping are common—for example, elderly people are viewed as wise, a man should be the breadwinner, and a woman, who is considered weak and needing to be looked after, the homemaker. Children are regarded as the true wealth of a family, especially the boys, who are supposed to provide for their parents when they grow old; young and unmarried girls should be shy and obedient. Strong family ties make people dependent upon each other, both economically and socially.

Everyone in Pakistan is friendly toward a foreigner, but it takes a while to develop true friendship. Within this hierarchical society, everyone tries to please those who are their superiors, either in the workplace or at home.

The Muslims of Pakistan believe strongly in their religion but they do not always practice it themselves. Culture trumps religion in certain parts of society, although few would admit it.

Most Pakistanis are passionate by nature, and are often committed to a cause, be it a friendship, a business venture, or a game. A normal discussion can turn into a heated debate. If the national cricket team wins an international match there will be public jubilation, but if it loses—the players are devils. There is a joke that for Pakistanis a game becomes war and war becomes a game. On the other hand, most Pakistanis believe in *kismet* (fate): failure is considered an act of God, and nobody takes responsibility for it. People console each other with the word *kismet* in any calamity, and counsel patience.

Esteem or status may be earned in different ways. A rich Pakistani may be regarded as successful, but true respect is reserved for other attributes. *Sayyeds*, the descendants of Prophet Mohammad, doctors, and teachers are more highly regarded than a rich person in some regions. A person—man or woman—who defends the honor of his or her family will also gain respect.

Work ethic is low in the government bureaucracy, where files move around offices for approvals and signatures. It is different in the private sector, which is more efficient. In a social context time is not money, but in private businesses time matters, and deadlines are met if there is no genuine reason for delays.

Most Pakistanis love to have guests, who, in Islam, are considered a *rahmat* (blessing) from God. Every foreigner is regarded as a guest, and is therefore received with warmth and open hearts (more on this in Chapter 4).

FAMILY TIES

The basis of both the social structure and individual identity is the extended family. This includes the nuclear family, immediate relatives, distant relatives, tribe members, friends, and neighbors. The word *khandaan* is often used to describe a family, and how many relatives are included in a *khandaan* varies from region to region. A complicated and extensive system of referring to relatives is in place, with titles to differentiate, for example, between maternal and paternal aunts. An average family household in Pakistan consists of at least eight persons, often with a number of close relatives living in one house.

It is common for a son to continue living with his parents and other siblings after his marriage. He and his wife will be given a separate bedroom, and the new bride will be expected to adjust to the household rules, obey her mother-in-law, and look after everyone. Millions of Pakistani men work overseas, while their wives stay at home, living with the extended family, often grandparents, uncles, and aunts. Sometimes the wife chooses to live with her own parents, which is acceptable.

Culturally, women are seen as inferior to men and are expected to be obedient to their husbands and other male members of the family. Women and girls are protected from outside influences, and it is considered inappropriate to ask about a wife or other female relatives when greeting someone. A female visitor will be asked inside the house to join the womenfolk, out of respect. Young women's health issues are secretly guarded and kept within the family by their mothers and aunts. Loyalty to the family comes before all other social relationships, and even business. This comes in handy at times of economic hardship, and money is borrowed for weddings, education, and even business, when necessary.

Children are an important part of the family, but they are to be seen and not heard. They are expected to be obedient, and their smart cousins are often held up as an example to them to work harder at their studies. Girls are considered ready for marriage at puberty, and if unmarried at thirty will be treated as old, and suitable only for a widower or a divorced man. Men, on the other hand, can take a wife at the age of eighty in certain circumstances. A widow can marry again if she is young, and this is regarded as good for her own protection. Orphans are generally looked after and supported by grandparents, and adoption rarely happens.

THE FEUDAL SYSTEM

The provinces of Sindh and Balochistan are largely feudal societies, where a few families own large areas of land, property, and other assets. The landlord, by virtue of his ownership and control of the land, is powerful enough to influence the distribution of water, fertilizers, tractor permits, and agricultural credit, and so exercises considerable influence over the revenue, police, and judicial administration of the area. This feudal elite has moved into politics, where it exerts a huge influence. As a result, the major political parties are feudal-oriented, and more than two-thirds of the National Assembly (lower house) are composed of this class. Also, most of the key executive posts in the provinces are held by them. The consequence of this feudal structure is a culture of nepotism, or *sifaresh* (recommendation), in which appointments are secured by indirect communication through those who can put pressure on officials for a favor. *Rishvat* (bribery) is also endemic. However, everyone loves to hate the two words *sifaresh* and *rishvat*.

Pakistani society is divided roughly into four groups, distinguished by deep economic differences:

- An extremely rich group (industrialists, feudal lords, and politicians), powerful through money, influence, and connections.
- The professional and skilled working classes, mostly living in the cities with connections to the villages through family or friends.
- Village dwellers, who mostly live off the land and agriculture, not necessarily poor, and in some cases educated.
- The business class, which includes both small and big businesses.

MULTILAYERED IDENTITIES

Every Pakistani belongs to an ethnic, linguistic, or religious group, which can sometimes be identified by the family name. The largest ethnic groups are

Punjabis, Sindhis, Pashtuns, and Baloch, concentrated in the four provinces. There are also groups based on language, the largest being the Urdu-speaking Muhajirs (migrants from India), Kashmiri, Balti, Saraiki, and Hindko, among others. Faith or religion-based groups are Shia, Sunni, Ismaili, Baha'i, Qadiyani, Christian, Hindu, and Sikh. Most Pakistanis are multilingual, and speak at least three languages, at times comfortably switching between them. These groupings are not that institutionalized, though some communities try to keep marriage within their own ethnic or religious group.

The caste system among the Muslims of Pakistan is known as *zat*, and some of the castes are actually professions adopted by families and passed down from generation to generation. For example a village barber (*nai*, or *naaee*), butcher (*qasab*), and clothes washer (*dhobi*) fall into these groups. With the spread of education, new professions are evolving, and groups are mixing through marriage.

There are strong stereotypical perceptions of the people of a region by those living outside that region. Conflict on the basis of ethnicity is not widespread, but it can become a problem, as in the case of Karachi, where recent years have seen targeted killings of the Pashtun and Muhajir groups. Religious conflicts occur between Shia and Sunni communities at the time of Ashura (see pages 45–46).

RELIGION

The majority of Pakistanis are Muslim by birth, and live according to the Five Pillars of Islam. They are relatively relaxed about their religious duties, however, and may not follow everything rigidly.

The Five Pillars of Islam are:
- Belief in God and the Prophet Mohammad.
- Praying five times a day, facing toward Makkah (Mecca).
- Fasting in the month of Ramadan, the ninth month of the lunar calendar.
- Giving a fixed portion of one's wealth to the needy.
- Going on *Hajj* (pilgrimage) once in one's lifetime, if one can afford it.

Azan, the call to prayer on loudspeakers from the mosques, can be heard five times a day in every city and village of the country. If you are visiting Pakistan for the first time, this can seem very noisy, especially if there are three mosques in your neighborhood. People generally stop playing music, and most women cover their heads out of respect. *Azan* is also recited softly into the ears of a newborn baby. "Haji" is a title for those who have performed *Hajj*, and they are respected by others.

A Muslim woman can remarry after the death of her husband, or divorce, and can return to her father's home if she wishes. Although Islam gives women the right of inheritance as well, this is seldom followed in Pakistan and the property usually goes to male members of the family. Having more than one wife is permitted in Islam, and is acceptable in Pakistani society, but is not prevalent.

PRAYERS AND MOSQUES

Pakistani Muslims say their prayers facing west to the Kaaba Mosque in the city of Makkah (Mecca), in Saudi Arabia. Men are supposed to go to the nearest mosque and women, in the mainstream Sunni tradition, pray at home. Pakistani Muslims respect the direction of prayer, the Qibla, so much that toilets are built to avoid facing it. Sprawling your feet toward the Qibla is regarded as rude, and beds are arranged in a room accordingly. It is common practice for a group of travelers to pray by the roadside near their bus or car. If you are traveling on public transportation, be prepared to have your journey broken for prayers.

Friday is the holy day, and most men try to go to the mosque for the afternoon *jumaa* (congregation). The weekend has been changed several times in Pakistan from Sunday to Friday and back again. People of the northwest and western parts of the country are stricter in saying their prayers, and local mosques there will normally be crowded with men. Most men take leave from work if they have to go to the mosque; business stops in some places. The local *imams* of the mosques are responsible for certain tasks, such as leading the prayers, or funeral prayers, the Friday *khutba* (sermon), and so on. In some communities food is regularly sent to local mosques, and the students who reside in those mosques for religious studies are provided with free meals from the neighborhood.

Visiting a Mosque

Before entering the mosques and shrines of the saints, you are required to take off your shoes. Ensure that you are respectably dressed and, if you are a woman, that your arms and ankles are covered, to avoid giving offense.

The Quran

The holy scripture of Islam is greatly revered, so that any small piece of paper with Arabic writing on it is sacred for ordinary Pakistanis. If they find such a scrap, it will immediately be picked up and put in a higher place out of respect. Copies of the Quran are found in every house, wrapped in several layers of elaborate cloth covering and kept on the highest shelf of the cupboard. Make sure that if you have a copy of the Quran, it is given due respect in Pakistan, and if you have an item of Arabic calligraphy, it should not be kept on the floor or at your feet. It should be wrapped and kept out of sight if possible.

Most Pakistani parents start their children's education at an early age by teaching them to recite

Arabic verses of the Quran as prayers. Boys are usually sent to the neighborhood mosque to read the Quran, whereas girls read it at home with a family member or female teachers. Some parents send their young children to special *madrassas* (religious schools) to learn to recite the Quran with the proper pronunciation, or even to learn it by heart. There will be Quran-reading sessions in which all thirty parts of the scripture are read in Arabic with no translation or explanation. Despite all this, very few Pakistanis understand the meaning of the written words in the Quran.

The Prophet

Pakistani Muslims believe in the *sunnah*, which means the way of the Prophet Mohammad, although it is not strictly practiced. The Prophet's birthday is celebrated with passion in *mehfil milad* (parties) by recitals of hymns (*hamd* and *naat*) without musical instruments. Great respect is shown to *sayyeds* (descendants of the Holy Prophet). They are greeted, addressed, and served first in a gathering, and in rural areas they have a lot of influence. The name Mohammad may be added to the name of a newborn boy as a prefix, for a blessing, and it is set in gold and worn around the neck.

Pakistan has a substantial number of Shia Muslims in all provinces who believe that the Prophet Mohammad's family and their descendants have special spiritual power. The martyrdom of the Prophet's grandson, Imam Hussain, is commemorated in the first Islamic month of Muharram. The tenth day, known as Ashura, is the day of mourning. Special meetings, recitals, and processions are arranged by the Shia community in

which Sunnis also take part. There are differences
of belief between the two about the transmission of
spiritual authority, and things can get nasty at the
time of Ashura in certain places.

Ramadan

During the holy month of Ramadan all healthy
Muslims must fast from dawn to dusk. Fasting
includes no eating, drinking, or smoking, and
people get up for breakfast before dawn. Waking the
sleepers is a noisy affair, and you may be disturbed
by the beating of drums in the streets at that time.
The opening hours of schools and offices are
adjusted accordingly; most restaurants are closed
during the day, but businesses function as usual.
Shops are usually open until late in the evenings,
and bazaars are busier than usual at that time. Those
who are exempted from fasting, such as the elderly,
or nursing mothers, do not eat or drink in public out
of respect to the others. It is a social taboo and a
crime in Pakistan under the Ramadan Ordinance
to drink, eat, or smoke in public, except for
travelers. Some businesses and hotels have special
arrangements for foreigners, and food is available on
request. At the end of Ramadan, Eid is celebrated
after the sighting of the new moon. (See page 58.)

Women and *Purdah*

Purdah is the concealment of women with a veil that
covers the face and body, and this can be seen in
many different shapes, colors, and materials.
Traditionally Pakistani women in agrarian societies
never covered their faces, although they wore a
shawl in winter over their heads and a cotton scarf
(*dupatta*) in the summer. Only the women of the

great feudal families wore some sort of veil as a status symbol. It is ironic that women from poor families start covering themselves when they become richer, and those from the upper class abandon the veil when they become more urbanized. Pakistan has a conservative form of Islam, with a fairly relaxed attitude toward women in Punjab and Sindh.

Since the beginning of the twenty-first century a new group of women wearing the Saudi *hijab*—covering hair, neck, and throat—has emerged, influenced by returning migrant workers. New fashionable and elaborate head covers can be seen in some cities. In the Pashtun areas, due to the threats of warring elements, some girls' colleges have introduced the *hijab* as a uniform, whereas in other areas women have taken refuge in the old-style *burqa* (shuttlecock-shaped shroud) for protection.

HONOR AND SHAME

Generally Pakistanis use the word *sharif* (respectable) to describe an honorable family, which could signify educated, wealthy, or with a feudal background. Making somebody publicly ashamed of an action in Pakistan could be seen as an insult to that person's honor. Similarly, if a person's honor is violated it will bring shame upon him. There are two more words used to define honor: *namoos* and *izzat*. In some societies, if a house is broken into and goods stolen this is considered a violation of honor rather than a loss of material items. The word *sharam* (shame) is used in everyday language, for example if a woman dresses indecently, or if a child fails an exam. The use of derogatory words, name-calling, or abusive language may all be considered a violation of honor, and taken very seriously. In some cultures having no honor has another meaning: for example, if a man's wife works in an office while he looks after the children at home, he will be considered to be without honor, and the word *beghairat* (shameless) will be used to describe him. The same word will be used for a wife beater in other cultures.

A woman is referred to as the *izzat* (honor) of the family, and if she behaves badly will be regarded as a threat to that honor. If a forced marriage fails, or if a woman is unable to have children, there may be divorce, but this is considered a matter for great family shame. In many communities divorce is still a taboo word, and women will allow their husbands to take another wife rather than get a divorce.

HOSPITALITY AND GENEROSITY

Pakistanis pride themselves on their tradition of hospitality, and on entering a house you will immediately be offered tea in winter and a cold (nonalcoholic) drink in the summer. Under the extended family system, relatives may stay over for days, even for weeks, without hesitation. Being tightfisted with a guest, even if uninvited, is unacceptable in some communities, and it is customary for a visitor to ask for a cup of tea or cold drink in the house of a friend or acquaintance. Every household is prepared to accommodate guests, and there is a proverb, "A guest and death can come without warning."

Most houses have a sitting room, used only when guests are entertained, known as a *baithak* (a place to sit). In some societies, a separate area close to the house is allocated for men, known as a *mehman khana* (guest house) or *hujra* (in Pashtun areas), or a *dera* (in Sindh and Balochistan).

The concept of a *musafir* (traveler or visitor) has the deeper meaning of one who needs compassion as well as shelter and food. In northern villages, a traveler from outside is regarded a guest of the whole village, and in some areas these guests are jealously guarded—sometimes perhaps too much, when, for example, a guest is not allowed to visit others without the approval of the host.

Gifts

Giving gifts is part of hospitality, and in some cultures those who are visiting for a first time must be given a gift when they leave. In daily life people are always helpful to each other, and the subtext for this generosity is the expectation of reciprocity. This happens in extended families as well as among friends. You look after your neighbor's elderly parent during the day, and your neighbor will give you a ride to the market for your weekly groceries. In rural communities all favors are remembered, and for example if someone is given money as a present on his wedding, he has to do the same in his turn, and even give more.

TOLERANCE AND PREJUDICE.

The Urdu word *rawadari* as used in Pakistan means tolerance, and it defines the underlying culture. Although Pakistan is an ethnically divided society, this does not cause conflict. Perhaps friends mock or ridicule another group in private conversations, but people speaking different languages and religious beliefs live comfortably side by side. However, marriages between various groups on the basis of compatibility, which could be social or economic, are common in big cities. There is prejudice about skin color, but it is not institutionalized or politicized. Men prefer to marry a fair woman, which is the standard of beauty in Pakistan.

Extramarital sex is considered a sin and a crime. Public displays of affection between a man and a woman are not tolerated, and boys and girls are not supposed to walk hand-in-hand, or kiss or hug in public. Homosexuality is illegal, considered a sin by the state as well as the public, and is therefore not acceptable (yet there is a traditional tolerated community of transvestites). Men, particularly boys, walk hand-in-hand or with arms around each other's shoulders—but in no way is this a sexual gesture.

ATTITUDES TO THE OUTSIDE WORLD

Anti-Indian sentiments and beliefs are widely held among many Pakistanis, yet Indian products, movies, and television dramas are favorites of the masses. Globalization has increased the influence of Western culture in Pakistan, especially among the affluent, who have easy access to new, expensive products. Many Western chain stores have been established in the major cities.

At the same time, there is also a reactionary movement within the country that wants to turn away from Western influence, and this has manifested itself in a return to traditional social and religious attitudes. Pakistan has lost many civilians in terror attacks, but it also has high levels of support for extremists in the population. This is an expression of anti-American or anti-Western sentiment, which has been inflamed by the Palestine issue, the burning of the Quran in Florida, and outrage over the Danish cartoon of the Prophet Mohammad. Kashmir is a particularly sensitive topic, and is best avoided.

Use common sense and a healthy dose of courtesy when in conversation with Pakistanis. Some people may not be tolerant of other religions, and a debate could turn nasty. If you do get involved in a discussion about religion, then remain respectful and positive rather than provocative and teasing. It is a common practice that in a group discussion, some Pakistanis will take your side because they do not want to offend a guest.

The more than seven million Pakistanis working abroad are generally admired in their motherland, and considered successful. They have sent home billions of dollars to their families. In fact overseas Pakistani workers, mainly in the Middle East, and all men, are the second-largest source of foreign exchange. They are not only admired, but sometimes envied because of their wealth.

ATTITUDES TO SUCCESS
Attitudes to success depend on factors such as regional culture and social norms, as well as on the perceptions of individuals and families. The definition

of success is also different in Pakistan, where people might feel proud to be related to a successful sportsman or a politician, but not to a film or TV star or a singer. The majority of the population loves music, and might show respect for such people in public, but they would not want to be related to them or have them as friends.

In a tribal society, a successful person might evoke envy among his relatives. Cousins can become enemies through feelings of resentment caused by one having more money or a better life.

Society is loosely divided according to the kinds of work and various professions, evolved over centuries. Craftsmen, for example, tended to be poor, and a person from a well-off family would never have learned to become a blacksmith or a potter. Today, however, young men who master such crafts are earning good money and are considered most successful.

WORK ETHIC

Due to lack of social support or a government benefit system, every family must have their men and sometimes their women working, not only to earn a livelihood but also to save for the future. Most Pakistanis try to get government jobs, which are usually for life, and which pay a pension after retirement. The best-paid government job is that of a bureaucrat. Like many bureaucrats in the world, Pakistanis will expand their work to fit in the time they have, and the way to do this is to do nothing and let the work pile up. Since no work gets done, a lot more work needs to be done. This has an added benefit. Those who need to get something done are then forced to grease palms. "A meeting," in governmental circles, is a euphemism for having tea with cronies.

There are people who do their work honestly, though most of them try to hide the fact that they actually do anything useful. The reason for this is to avoid resentment from their colleagues, recruited through recommendations (*sifarish*), and usually incapable or incompetent. The permanent employees of the government hold on to their positions even if they are incompetent, because they have been selected through a competitive Civil Service exam.

ATTITUDES TO TIME

Most Pakistani workers do not waste their time, and find innovative ways to make or spend more money. Teachers provide private tuition in the evenings to compensate for their low salaries, doctors have private clinics, and an office worker might help in the family shop after work. This becomes an abuse when a teacher goes to his school once a month to get his salary, or a doctor working in a government clinic or hospital asks patients to go to his private clinic in the evening to be treated for a fee.

In government jobs there are many excuses for coming late to work, or for not appearing at all. If Friday is not a day off, employees might disappear for the midday prayers, and nobody would stop them. In the fasting month of Ramadan some people habitually turn up late for work and then by midday they all fall apart, incapable of doing any work. Funerals and sickness are common excuses, and the official four days off when a public holiday is merged with the weekend can easily become six or even eight days. However, workers in the private sector and businesses are more conscientious, as they lose wages or even their job for not showing up at work.

ATTITUDES TO EDUCATION

Pakistanis use the Arabic word *taaleem* to mean education, but this is not as comprehensive as it sounds. If somebody can simply read and write, he or she is *taaleem yafta*, or "the one who has got education," and very few people believe in study for the sake of gaining knowledge. Most Pakistanis want to educate their children for better employment opportunities. A common phrase used in Urdu translates to "after reading and writing, have a good job." There is a perception that private, fee-paying schools provide "good education," and many parents believe that if their child goes to a private school, he will have a better chance in his future life, not necessarily because of their knowledge but because his classmates will be the children of the elite class, where everyone wants to be. As a result, private schooling is becoming more popular, and some parents are using all their resources to pay the fees.

In the rural areas, formal school education is still considered suitable only for clever children and due to poverty many parents would want their sons to be able to earn money rather than study. Another Arabic word, *madrassa*, which literally means "school," is commonly used for religious seminaries throughout Pakistan. Usually the very poor will send their sons to these *madrassas* if they provide free boarding and meals.

There is a new, more religious elite class appearing in Pakistan that wants their children to study Islam along with other subjects of the national curriculum. There is now a chain of more modern fee-paying schools that follow a strict discipline of Islamic studies. They are mixed at primary level, and the girls wear Arabic-style *hijabs*.

Most people in Pakistan believe that a little education, perhaps up to secondary level, is enough for a girl. If she is going to get married and live in someone else's house, why waste money and time on higher education? Parents of an eligible bachelor usually look for a young bride of seventeen to twenty years of age. Even educated parents prefer to have their daughters engaged before they graduate (normally at the age of nineteen). Some girls do not complete their school education, and many drop out of higher education. It is usually perceived that the young women who go to university are cleverer, and may not be able to run a household successfully. The ones who complete higher education and get a job are considered not only clever but also emancipated, and a common perception is that they may use their knowledge as a leverage to be independent.

CUSTOMS &
TRADITIONS

Pakistan is a conservative country, where men and woman usually wear traditional loose, baggy trousers and knee-length shirts (*shalwar-kamees*). You will notice that men wear sober hues, such as gray, blue, black, brown, or white, but women will be seen in all sorts of beautiful colors, with matching accessories. Very few men wear Western-style trousers for everyday wear, but on formal occasions they prefer to wear a suit. A moustache is still considered a sign of manliness, and a beard denotes piety—though it has become a necessity in some areas for security. The first-time visitor will notice that there is a large cultural and economic gap between the social classes. Sometimes it can be seen in the condition of a person's dress or physique, or the expression on his or her face.

Self-expression finds an outlet in traditional art in transport throughout Pakistan. Taxis, buses, auto rickshaws, and trucks are customized with lurid colors, shiny attachments, tiny mirrors, and lights.

Seasonal and religious festivals, along with old, pre-Islamic beliefs, keep all communities busy with various rituals throughout the year. The end of winter, the harvests, fasting, attending special prayers, and anniversaries of important saints are all celebrated with zeal and passion. There is an amalgamation of ethnic cultures that either overlap in neighboring areas or differ completely according to the climate and geography. From eating habits to the structure of houses, and from attire to recreation, there are many shades of vibrant color.

Social life is simple in Pakistan, with an Islamic touch as well as unusual ancient beliefs. Non-Muslims—Christians, Hindus, Sikhs, and Buddhists—also have a mixture of local and faith-based traditions. The official calendar in Pakistan is Gregorian, but the Islamic lunar calendar is followed for the religious festivals.

PUBLIC HOLIDAYS

Six public holidays are celebrated each year:

February 5: Kashmir Solidarity Day, to protest against Indian occupation of Kashmir

March 23: Commemoration of the passing of the Pakistan Resolution in 1940, when the demand for a separate country was made by the Muslims of India

May 1: Labor Day

August 14: Independence Day

September 11: Anniversary of the death of the founder of Pakistan, Muhammad Ali Jinnah

December 25: Birthday of Muhammad Ali Jinnah

There are a number of days that are important for the military and the establishment, which have little effect on the population, such as November 9, the birthday

of the national poet Iqbal, which is marked in official circles and given special media coverage. Various other public holidays may be declared, and visitors are advised to check these on the current yearly calendars.

THE ISLAMIC YEAR

The Islamic calendar consists of twelve lunar months, making a year of 354 days, so the dates of religious festivals move in relation to the Western Gregorian calendar.

THE LUNAR MONTHS

1.	Muharram	7.	Rajab
2.	Safar	8.	Shaaban
3.	Rabi-ul-Awwal	9.	Ramadan
4.	Rabi-ul Thani	10.	Shawwal
5.	Jumada-ul-Awwal	11.	Zul-Qaadah
6.	Jumada-ul-Thani	12.	Zul-Hajj

Eid-Ul-Fitr

This is the biggest holiday for the masses in Pakistan, and is known as "small Eid." It marks the end of the fasting month of Ramadan, when the new

moon is sighted. There is a three-day public holiday, and preparations are made weeks in advance. Shops are decorated, and people buy new clothes and shoes. Most Pakistanis wear tailor-made clothes, and Ramadan is the busiest time for the tailors, though in the big cities ready-made *shalwar-kamees* are sold, which can also be pricey. Women buy new bangles and other ornaments for the occasion.

The evening of the sighting of the moon is full of activity, both in and outside the house. Women and children apply henna to their hands, sweets are bought, gifts are sent to newly married or engaged women, and plans for visiting families are finalized. On the day of Eid prayers are offered by the men in *eidgah* (special large open-air mosques) and other vast grounds. A special dish of *siwayyan* (vermicelli cooked with milk and sugar) is eaten, and the young pay their respects to the senior members of the extended family. Children are given a little money, known as *eidee*, and the day is spent in socializing and eating a variety of foods.

Eid-Ul-Adha

This is the second big celebration, known as big Eid," marking the completion of Hajj. After special prayers in the *eidgah*, cows, goats, or rams are slaughtered, by those who can afford it, in commemoration of the Prophet Ibrahim's willingness to sacrifice his son. The sacrificial meat is divided into three parts: one for the poor, one for relatives, and a third for one's own consumption.

The Birthday of the Prophet Mohammad

This is celebrated on the twelfth day of the month of Rabi-ul-Awwal. Special processions are arranged in the cities, with the distribution of sweets and food. Big city councils arrange processions with beautiful floats and recitations of *naat* (religious poems) by men and children.

Muharram
The first month of the Islamic calendar, Muharram, marks the martyrdom of Imam Hussain, grandson of the Prophet Mohammad. People of the Shia sect have special gatherings to commemorate the event, and Sunni Muslims also join the processions and other rituals.

SEASONAL FESTIVITIES
Pakistan, we have seen, is a nation of migrants, and there are as many local festivals as there are ethnic and linguistic groups. The ancient nomadic Aryan tradition celebrating the end of winter is still a part of Pakistani culture. Every region has its festivals, based on anything from horse and cattle trading to foods, with music and dance attracting large numbers of people. The word for these events is *mela*, which originally meant "to meet," and is still

used throughout the country for local folk celebrations. The summer months are marked by the wheat harvest, and communities come together in the fields to help. With the new agro-technology, old practices have died out, but rural areas are still hubs of activity at harvest time. There are village fetes, with local games, competitions, wrestling, and *kabadi*, a local team game. In the cities, traditional fairs have been replaced by agriculture, flower, and industrial exhibitions, book fairs, streets of food stalls, and mango fairs. Local colleges arrange *meena bazar* (fairs) on their grounds for a day of entertainment with food and handicraft stalls. Every region and ethnic group has its own traditions for local festivals.

Balochistan

Tribal Balochi society has numerous colorful events. The Sibi festival, with its ancient roots, attracts people from across the province. Numbers of local cattle are brought here for trade, and it is the place to see and appreciate the best breeds of livestock.

Camel and horse displays, folk-dance groups, music performances, craft stalls, cattle shows, and other entertainments present a dazzling riot of color. A peculiar game showing strength and horsemanship is *buzkashi*, in which two teams of five players compete on horseback to snatch and gain control of a goat carcass.

The Gulestan Mela and Pishin Mela were two traditional fairs, held as recently as twenty years ago; unfortunately both have become a victim of the Afghan war and insecurity in this border area.

Punjab

Winter ends in February in Punjab and the southern parts of the country, and the festival of *Basant*, one of the popular celebrations of Punjab, is celebrated with kite flying and open-air parties. The yellow mustard blooms in this season, and yellow is considered the color of spring. Women wear yellow clothes and enjoy themselves on swings and in the traditional circular dance known as *luddi*. In the cities, kite battles and brawls are common scenes outside in the streets, and there are rooftop parties with loud music.

The National Horse and Cattle Show is held at the end of February or the beginning of March in Lahore Fortress Stadium. There are races, trained cattle dances, tent pegging, a tattoo show, folk music, bands, games, and cultural floats. The show has been described as an eloquent expression of Pakistan's heritage and an authentic demonstration of its agricultural and industrial achievements.

There are several other occasions, including Mela Chiraghan (the festival of lamps) and other *urs* (death anniversaries of saints) at the main shrines of Lahore, Multan, and Pakpattan, to name but a few.

Sindh

The province of Sindh is the land of Sufi saints, and their tombs are a hub of activity at the time of *urs*,

which is usually the celebration of a Sufi's life. The seventeenth-century Sindhi poet Shah Abdul Latif Bhitai is revered in this region as a Sufi saint and his *urs* is celebrated in the second month of the Islamic calendar (on 14 Safar) for three days. There are open markets with plentiful stalls of food and local handicrafts that attract thousands from the neighboring villages and other parts of the country.

Another famous *urs* is that of the saint and poet Shahbaz Qalandar in Sehwan in the month of Shaban. The city springs to life and becomes the focal point of more than half a million pilgrims from all over Pakistan. This three-day festival is celebrated with *qawwali* music, folk music, and the Sufi dance known in the local language as *dhamal*.

Annual spring celebrations are marked with horse and cattle shows in the cities of Jacobabad and Larkana. Jashn-i-Shikarpur is also the celebration of spring, marked with music, dance, and folk art.

Khyber Pakhtunkhwa

The spring season is marked with a number of festivals and *melas* in the villages of the northwest. A large number of Afghan refugees celebrate the Afghan New Year on March 21 with picnics and social gatherings. In the provincial capital city Peshawar and surrounding areas, the ancient traditional Jhanday (flag festival) in April has not taken place for more than fifteen years—a victim of the continuing conflict on its borders.

A new spring festival was recently established, arranged by the provincial government. Known as Jashn-e-Baharan, it takes place near the Kabul River at Kund for three days in the last week of March. The main interest is in food pavilions, and there is an air show and fireworks that attract crowds of locals. Jashn-i-Khyber is an industrial exhibition with food, theater, music, and craft fairs.

Other activities, such as polo matches, tent pegging, and shooting take place throughout the year. At Dera Ismail Khan, local games, folk dances, music, races for horses, buffaloes, and even dogs, and exhibitions of handicrafts are popular. These events happen only when there is relative peace in the area.

Northern Areas

The most important seasonal festival is Nauroz, the Zoroastrian New Year, on March 21, celebrated in Gilgit, Hunza, Skardu, and Chitral. This features polo, football, volleyball, and hockey matches, folk dances, and music. The Shandur Polo Festival, between the teams of Chitral and Gilgit, is held in May on the highest polo ground in the world, on Shandur Pass.

Between May and July the northern areas of the country are the focus of traditional fairs now patronized by the government. Two other events, welcoming spring and a harvest festival, are celebrated in the Kalash Valleys, and attract tourists from all over Pakistan. They are locally known as Chelum Josht (May) and Ucchal (August). Phoo, the September grape harvest festival, and Chomos, an event in December remembering the dead, also take place locally.

Islamabad

The capital city is busy during the summer months with a variety of stage and fashion shows. The Lok Virsa (National Institute of Folk and

Traditional Heritage) arranges a number of events throughout the year. There is a folk festival with music contests, dancing, and craftsmen at work, and an exhibition and sale of handicrafts. These events present a rare opportunity to see the culture and craft of the whole of Pakistan in one place.

The National Industrial Exhibitions, at which big companies from all over the country exhibit their products in Lahore to pitch for businesses and deals, also provide an opportunity to see and buy national products and handicrafts.

LITERARY ACTIVITIES

Pakistan has a rich tradition of storytelling, and even in this time of new technology people love to tell stories to each other in a group. In rural societies storytellers and poets are still held in high regard. Evenings are for leisure, and people get together in a field or under a tree and talk about the events of the day in story form.

Poetry is a deeply respected art. The enthusiasm for poetry exists at a regional level as well, with nearly all of Pakistan's provincial languages continuing the legacy, in a mix of Hindi and Persian formats. In some regions epic poetry is accompanied by stringed instruments as a popular form of entertainment for men. The poetry recitals are known as *mushaira*, in which poets present their latest work to a live audience.

Pakistani Urdu poetry contains elements of other regional languages. Poetry in the form of religious hymns (*marsia*, *salam*, and *naath)* is appreciated. Sometimes, a poem will depict the political situation in satirical form, which is an expression of frustration.

There are a number of small literary clubs and societies throughout the country, where local poets and writers get together.

WEDDINGS

Weddings, which are boisterous events with loud music, dancing, and food, are a great source of entertainment for Pakistanis. They provide an opportunity to socialize and see new fashions in dresses and jewelry, and to assess young men and girls as prospective marriage partners. Even poor families have two- to three-day celebrations.

In the first and most colorful and noisy party of the celebrations, relatives of both families apply *mehndi* (henna paste) to their hands in intricate

patterns. The bride, usually wearing a yellow or green dress, is encircled by women who apply the henna to her hands and feet. The bridegroom will have a tiny amount on his palm or little finger.

In some places, the marriage vows (*nikah*) take place on the same day. This is a simple ceremony, with a religious man reading verses from the Quran, and two witnesses, one from the bride's family and one from the groom's. The consent of both the bride and the groom should be clearly heard as a "yes," and completes the ceremony. Written contracts, which are signed after the religious ceremony, are used in the cities.

The *barat* (wedding procession) is usually the main event, in which the splendidly dressed bridegroom, along with his family and friends, goes to the bride's house and, after a meal or refreshments, takes the bride back to his own family house. This is called the *rukhsati* (farewell) of the bride, who usually wears a red dress embroidered with gold or silver threads and a variety of beads. The *valima* (reception) is either the next day or a few days later at the bridegroom's house.

Close relatives make preparations for the whole affair months in advance, and after the wedding, videos and photographs of the ceremonies are shown with pride to all. As a result of the growing numbers of elaborate weddings, a whole industry has formed in the big cities in the past few years, with purpose-built wedding halls, beauty parlors, and car decorations. Fabrics, embroidery, trimmings, flowers, candles, lamps, sweets, and other delicacies are all essentials for a Pakistani wedding.

The majority of marriages are still arranged by parents or elders in the extended family, though this is changing in the cities. Traditionally, first or second cousins are matched, and in some communities it is still the practice for baby girls to be promised in marriage. A dowry or bride price may be demanded, depending on the area. However, with the spread of education, economic independence, and urbanization, these traditions are changing. Forced marriages, against the will of the bride or groom, are not uncommon, but the dowry system varies from region to region. Urdu-speaking Muhajirs and Punjabis expect, and in some cases demand, huge dowries from the bride's family. In Pashtun and Balochi culture the bridegroom is expected to pay dowry money to the bride's father as well as covering the expenses of the wedding feast.

CELEBRATING AT HOME

A number of local and traditional events are celebrated in all regions, with special food or other rituals. The fifteenth day of the Islamic month of Shaaban is marked with fireworks in some places.

The pilgrimage of Hajj is considered the most important journey of a lifetime, and when someone returns from Mecca, family and friends welcome him or her with garlands of flowers.

Throughout the country the birth of a male child is greeted with rejoicing, music, and singing. Sweets are distributed in the neighborhood. A little money or some sweets are immediately given to the person who carries the news of a first-born boy to close relatives. In some cultures people will rejoice by shooting in the air. In contrast, the birth of a girl is a low-key affair and close relatives simply wish her parents good *naseeb* (fortune).

The first shaving of a baby's head (*aqiqa*) is marked by the sacrifice of a goat. This is done for both a boy and a girl. The circumcision of boys, a baby's first teeth, and the first steps are all cause for celebration within the family. Success in an important exam, getting a new job, starting a new business, and the arrival of a son or daughter from a foreign country are all celebrated with a special family meal. Birthdays are celebrated only in more modern and Westernized families.

FAMILY VISITS

Very few Pakistanis choose to live alone, and elderly parents are considered the responsibility of their children. Family obligations are important, and it is essential to keep the ties strong by visiting the extended family and relatives. If someone is ill, they must be visited in the hospital or at home. Someone who passes an important exam, gets a job, or starts a new business must also have visits from close relatives.

After the greetings, which are either in the local language or the Islamic *Assalamualaikum* (peace be upon you) and *Alekumslam* (and to you), men shake hands or hug. Women don't shake hands, and hug only other women (three times). To show respect to an elderly visitor, women cover their heads and men stop smoking.

A visit usually begins with inquiries about the health of the children and family members, and then conversation moves on to the latest events and other topics. Sweets, or even sugar, may be brought to mark happy events, and the visitor must congratulate the host. Fruit or flowers are brought to the ill, and money is given discreetly to the head of a bereaved family. Short visits usually last for a couple of hours. The visitors are given tea or other refreshments, and the hosts will insist that they stay for a meal, which the visitors politely refuse.

Neighbors are treated as family: there is in fact a Punjabi proverb that says a neighbor is like one's own mother's child. Borrowing and lending from neighbors, sharing special dishes, and asking for help is common in day-to-day life.

FUNERALS

For most Pakistanis, a person dies when his or her time is up, and nobody can change that time. Therefore the phrase, "untimely death" does not apply. Showing extreme grief is common, especially by women, and other women may join in to show sympathy with the bereaved. Men do not generally shed tears in public, but if they do, it is not regarded as abnormal.

Every household in the extended family must be represented at the funeral, which is also attended by neighbors and friends. The body is washed and cleaned according to Islamic rituals, and wrapped in a white, unstitched, cotton shroud. Men offer special prayers in open ground, and everyone nearby will join in. Contrary to other religions, where a coffin is usually carried slowly, a Muslim's body is hurried to the graveyard after the prayers. While it is being taken to the graveyard, male passersby will also try to shoulder the coffin, or walk a few paces with it, to fulfill their Islamic obligation.

Men take leave from their work to attend a funeral. It is quite acceptable if somebody is absent from even a very important meeting for this reason; in some circumstances the meeting can be canceled altogether, and if you happen to be present it is better to attend the funeral with the others, though this is not an obligation.

The eldest male member of a family will be receiving mourners for *fateha* (condolence) in his house, which is an important family obligation. Neighbors and near relatives send cooked food, tea, and other refreshments to the bereaved family for a few days. Normally, mourners stay for a short while after the funeral but do not eat or drink. However, in hot weather, drinking water or fruit juice drinks is acceptable, and food may be offered if people have come from a distance.

On the third day of the funeral prayers are offered, followed by distribution of food to the poor. The tenth day (*daswan*) and every Thursday till the fortieth day (*chehlum*) are all marked with special prayers and food distribution to the poor. The most Westernized, modern elite do not follow these rituals strictly, and others may not follow because of economic hardship.

FOLKLORE AND SUPERSTITION

Many areas of Pakistan are influenced by Hindu and Buddhist culture, and share common superstitions with India. The arrival of guests heralded by a crow, and the crying of cats at night are considered unlucky. One shoe on top of the other means imminent traveling. Giving sharp items like knives, scissors, or needles is unlucky, and heralds imminent argument, fight, or a conflict, and such items, if borrowed, should always be returned immediately after use.

Some rituals are modified and attached to religion. For example, when someone is leaving the house on a long journey, the women of the family will bring a copy of the Quran and hold it above the traveler's head for a safe journey. A similar tradition is followed when a bride leaves her parents' house at the time of her wedding. When she arrives at her husband's house, a goat or cock will be slaughtered at her feet to ward off evil. A small knife or sharp item is kept under the pillow of a newborn baby to keep evil spirits away. Some people sprinkle water on the threshold when a visitor leaves the house.

Kismet

Most Pakistanis believe in fate, or *kismet*. Good or bad fortune is regarded as the will of God. People who die due to negligence in hospital, the wrong dose of medicine, or lack of health facilities are mourned, but everyone believes that it was just bad luck, and the will of God, that the person should die in that way.

Many people want to know what lies in the future, or in their *kismet*. If they can think they can ward off or change the course of a misfortune through prayer or special offerings in a shrine, they will try to do so. Palmists, soothsayers, and *najumis* (astrologers) are contacted when somebody has a problem or dilemma in their life.

Mannat and Shrines

A large number of Pakistanis, especially women, believe in the power of local saints, and will visit their shrines at a time of a misfortune in the family. There is a hierarchy of shrines, and some saints are known for their special powers.

A *mannat* is a wish made, usually in a famous shrine, often along with an obligation to fulfill. The obligation could be as small as putting oil in the lamps of the shrine, or distributing bread, or

as big as donating money for painting the shrine's walls. Failure to fulfill the obligation means that something tragic will happen to the person or their family. You might see people tying threads to the grille of a shrine, or putting a lock on it, as a reminder of their obligation. Special offerings of flowers, sweets, or a covering for the saint's grave may also be part of the obligation. On Thursdays, it is a common practice to offer food to the poor around the shrine.

The *Nazar*

Pakistanis are usually worried about jealousy, and special measures are taken for protection against evildoers. Many people believe in the *nazar* (evil eye), and it is part of everyday conversation.

There are several protective rituals: for example, because the color black is sacred, it has the power to ward off the evil eye, so a beautiful baby may have a black mark put on his forehead, and a big house may have a black flag on the top floor.

When somebody is struck by the evil eye, red chilies are burned in the stove of their house. Children carrying small tin containers with red-hot charcoal and hand fans, burning *harmal* plant seeds, are a common sight around bus or train stations; the seeds release a fragrant smoke that is regarded to have power against the evil eye. Some people will waft this smoke around the head of a newly wedded bride or bridegroom for protection against the gaze of strangers. Special amulets are hung around the neck for protection, and coral or cowries may be sewn into a child's hat or collar. You might find strange amulets and charms hanging from the rearview mirror of a car or a bus, usually to ward off the evil eye.

Jinns

The presence of *jinns*, which are supernatural creatures of free will, is believed in by most Pakistanis on the grounds that they are mentioned in the Quran. Islamic scholars do not usually deny their existence, but there are different views and interpretations.

Jinns have become part of the folklore, and any strange phenomenon may be attributed to their presence in everyday life. Like humans, they can be good or bad. *Jinns* can fall in love with a young girl and not let anyone else marry her, and any odd behavior, such as fits of anger or a psychological condition, particularly in a pretty girl, may be explained as possession by these beings. To remove them, a group of specialists known as *aamels* will be consulted. Sadly, a number of mental illnesses are attributed to the action of *jinns*.

Sadka and *Taveez*

There is a general belief in Pakistan that a tragedy can be averted by sacrificing a goat or a sheep and distributing the meat to the poor—a charitable act known as *sadka* (Arabic, alms, or handout). This is usually done when somebody survives an accident or is seriously ill, and the sacrifice of the head of an animal is thought to be a substitute for life. Alternatively, *sadka* money can be circled around the head of the person and then given to the poor. The word is also used poetically to show doting love, in Urdu and other regional languages: *mein tumharay sadkay*, for example, means "I give my life for you."

A *taveez* (amulet) usually consists of a prayer, a Quranic verse, or mystical numbers written on a small piece of paper and sewn up in a tiny leather pouch or enclosed in a silver shell. These amulets are worn around the neck or tied as armbands for protection. They are prepared and sold by specialists (*aamel*) who are believed to have particular spiritual power or authority to do so. An *aamel* may be a *peer* (religious figure). Even educated people believe that having Quranic verses in an amulet does no harm to the individual and can be worn for protection. If you are traveling on the Grand Trunk Road in Pakistan from south to north, you can't miss the writing on walls advertising these specialists and providing telephone numbers. A farmer might hang a special amulet around the neck of his bull to keep it healthy and protected.

An amulet could be good or bad, and it is up to the individuals to get the ones they need. Although dabbling in magic and putting a curse on somebody is strictly against Islamic belief, some people, out of jealousy, may use *taveez* to harm an enemy. This is more common in rural areas and, needless to say, the *aamels* make good money from such practices.

Jadoo, Toona-Totka

These words are equivalent to witchcraft, or casting spells, and the extreme form is known as *kala jadoo* (black magic). The west Punjab and Sindh provinces were under the influence of the *hindu tantrik* culture, and people in the rural areas believe in and sometimes practice it with bad intentions. It is believed that *jadoo* can make a person seriously ill or deformed through an ailment or an accident. Those who practice *jadoo* charge a lot of money, sometimes beyond the means of an ordinary Pakistani, hence it is not very common.

A mild form of magic is known as *toona-totka*, in which ordinary people come up with a few tricks. It is closely related to evil eye, and those who believe in these tricks will get the antidotes in the form of a *taveez* from a local *peer*, or make an offering at a shrine to break the spell.

chapter four

MAKING FRIENDS

Pakistan has a culture of warm friendliness, following the traditions of South Asia. People will generally greet you with enthusiasm if you approach them, and you don't need a formal introduction before having a conversation with a stranger, who will usually show you extraordinary kindness and goodwill on the very first meeting. English is widely spoken in the major cities and the business community, and the Islamic code of conduct is generally relaxed. Pakistanis are passionate about keeping friendship going with regular visits and communications, and the same will be expected from you.

FRIENDSHIP

Friendship, to a Pakistani, means a long-lasting relationship, and the word has both masculine and feminine forms in all the languages of the region. In Urdu, the word *dost* is used for a male friend and *saheli* for woman. Traditionally, friendship happens in the same gender with the same age group. A thirty-year old woman will not consider a forty-year-old woman as her friend, but as an older sister. The same applies to a man, who would even call his senior friend by a title meaning "big brother" out of respect. Modern and affluent circles, where a woman can have a man friend, may use *dost* for both genders. Childhood friends are generally treated as family members, and several generations will keep the relationship intact.

In traditional Pakistani society friendship does not mean a casual relationship or a passing acquaintanceship between individuals. If somebody is described as "my friend," it implies affection and loyalty. It can be a word of some strength, to mean the opposite of "enemy." The friend is always on your side, whatever you say or do. Friendship requires commitment and communication by both parties, and people are quickly offended if you don't keep in touch.

MAKING CONVERSATION

It is easy to start a conversation with a man in Pakistan if you are a man, and similarly as a woman it will be easy for you to have a casual conversation with another woman, in both formal and informal situations. Despite the variety of languages and dialects, *Assalamualaikum* (peace be upon you) with an extended hand is enough to start small talk. Generally, people respond positively to this greeting and are genuinely happy to hear it from a foreigner. English is understood and spoken by most of the elite, city dwellers, and shopkeepers. Pakistanis are naturally curious, and will at some point ask your nationality. If you are looking for an address or asking for directions in a street, you will be probably be escorted to your destination by the first person you ask. You can ask a Pakistani man as many questions as you wish, and he will happily supply not only the information but also some useful tips to show goodwill.

There are no specific places to go to socialize or meet people, unless through another friend or acquaintance. You have to keep an open mind and have good interpersonal skills to approach people. Some of the less personal topics of conversation are cricket, food, clothes, shopping, and the places you want to visit or have already visited. Subjects such as religion and fundamentalism could be difficult and are best avoided.

It is also possible to get to know people through social networks like Facebook and Twitter. The exchange of information about personal interests and business, along with their command of language, will reveal the status of a person. If you are a woman, it is better to have a conversation with a Pakistani woman first. Most educated women speak English. If you want to be bold, there is no harm in talking to men, but be aware of unwanted attention or mixed messages.

NOT SO PRIVATE

It is common practice in Pakistan to scrutinize a foreigner by gazing and staring out of curiosity. This can become uncomfortable at times, but be patient, because often people want to have a conversation but simply cannot express themselves. Don't be surprised by personal questions that your Pakistani partners or colleagues ask. They may ask about your age, marital status, and number of children, and be generally interested in your personal and family life. They want to get to know you, and it is best to answer them. Questions are restricted to male family members only, because discussing women in public is not considered appropriate.

Everyone wants to know whether you are married or single, and you can't stop further questions by answering! If you are single, they want to know why. If you are married, they want to know if you have children. If you say yes, they want to know how many boys and how many girls. If you say no, they want to know why not. It goes on and on. The best thing is either to have a plausible story or turn the table by asking questions yourself. A good tactic is to ask about their own family, and once they turn to children, they will happily tell you all about them.

Most Pakistanis would not disclose their own earnings to anyone, but some people might ask you casually how much you are earning, which foreigners find strange. You can politely decline to reply if you do not want to disclose this.

ATTITUDES TOWARD FOREIGNERS

Generally, Pakistanis are polite and helpful to foreigners. With access to Internet technology and awareness of other countries, young people in particular are enthusiastic to know more about other cultures. There is a fascination with modern ways of living, and young educated men, especially, will eagerly take the opportunity either to speak English with you or to find out about job prospects in your country.

There are preconceived ideas about various nationalities. For example, some Pakistani men believe that all European white women are easily

available for a relationship. The British and
Americans are considered snobs, the Chinese
disciplined, and the Central Asians tough. Arabs
are thought of as rich and arrogant; Turks are
considered to be friends.

There is a hidden suspicion of Westerners that
has escalated since 9/11 and the "war on terror."
In the Pashtun tribal areas along the border with
Afghanistan, white-skinned people are regarded as
infidels and not to be trusted. Despite the tradition
of hospitality and warmth, those who entertain
foreigners in these areas, or who may be close to
them, are suspected of being their agents. There is
a different attitude in the cities, where educated
people treat foreigners as guests. Men like to take
photographs with them; however they don't expect
their women to be photographed. As a woman
visiting a family you must ask for permission to
take a photo, and it's usually granted.

Most Pakistani men will treat a foreign woman
with the utmost respect, and in some cultures they
won't look at her directly, or will lower their eyes
when speaking to her. Sometimes, however, a
Western woman may be approached as if she were
easily available for sex.

INVITATIONS HOME

Pakistanis love inviting foreigners to their homes,
and will passionately tell them about their culture
and traditions. If you get an invitation for a meal,
the chances are that you will not be the only
guest, as your host will want to entertain you by
introducing you to his or her friends. If you are a
man visiting a family, don't expect to meet the

women of the household as well. If you are a woman, you are expected to sit in the *zenana* (the inner part of the house).

A man should not shake hands with a Pakistani woman unless she extends her hand to you. However, as a female you may shake hands with other women right away, or hug them if you want. It is common to receive warm and close hugs from your hosts, as if you were an old friend or relative, even if you are meeting them for the first time. Arrive approximately fifteen minutes later than the stipulated time when invited to dinner or a small gathering.

It is best to dress conservatively if it is your first visit to the house. As a woman you should wear a head scarf, which will please your host. Show respect for elders by greeting them first. On arrival, check to see if your host is wearing shoes, and, if not, remove yours at the door. The sitting area is probably carpeted, so you won't need slippers, but some will be provided if you want to go to the bathroom.

Although modern people and city dwellers eat their meals Western-style, at a table, ordinary Pakistani families sit on the floor for their meals. In some rural areas, it is common to eat meals from a knee-high round table while sitting on the floor. All the food is served at once; there are no courses. Many people don't use eating utensils—although the more Westernized families do—and a fork and spoon may be provided for a foreigner, but no knives are used, and meat is torn using the spoon. Guests are served first, and then others in order of seniority, continuing in an approximation of age order. Choose what you like, put it on your plate, and make sure that everyone else is served before you start eating. Don't use your left hand for eating or drinking, as it is considered unclean.

Normally the hostess will not sit to eat with the rest of the group but will hover over the company to check that there is plenty of food and to replenish the dishes. Pakistanis are very hospitable, and you will be urged to take second and even third helpings. Saying "I'm full" will be taken only as a polite gesture, and not taken at face value. Finishing a meal involves a delicate balance: cleaning your plate will invite more to be served, while leaving too much may signal that you didn't care for it. Aim at leaving just a little, announcing you're full, and strongly praising the food. In some cultures, your host will be watching your plate, serving you everything even if you do not want it, and will keep giving you more despite your protests. If you are unsure, watch what your Pakistani counterparts do.

If you have not met the women of the family and want to please your host, offer thanks to the person who has cooked the meal, either directly, if she is present, or through a male member of the family.

If you want to return the hospitality, you can say, "Do visit us when you are in my country," which means an invitation for a meal. Don't offer there and then to invite somebody to a restaurant, and don't make the mistake, as some foreigners do, of using the phrase, "buying a meal." This sounds strange in a Pakistani context, and may be thought offensive, implying need or poverty. If you invite someone for a meal and they turn up with a few friends, don't be surprised—they probably want to include you in their larger circle.

GIVING AND RECEIVING GIFTS

Pakistan has a rich culture of hospitality, and the giving of gifts is an essential part of that culture; it is a gesture to remind the visitor of the host, and also an act of reciprocity. A gift has different meanings in all societies of Pakistan, and its value shows how much honor has been given to a person. A shawl, hat, or something to wear means high respect; sweets are an indication of sharing joy; a cooked dish shows affection; a piece of jewelry, carpet, or similar items for the house indicates closeness. In some cultures, foreign visitors are not expected to give gifts to the host, although it is appreciated if they do.

If you are invited to someone's home, bring the hostess a small gift such as flowers or good-quality chocolates or sweets. Men should avoid giving flowers to women, and if a man must give a gift to a woman, he should say that it is from his wife, or mother, or sister. Do not give alcohol unless you know your host very well and that it will be appreciated. Give the gift using both hands. Most Pakistanis, out of politeness, don't show appreciation or excitement upon receiving a gift. It may seem strange to you, but this is considered vulgar. Sometimes, your host will put away the gift casually without even thanking you. This is not rudeness but dignity, and shows that they care more for you than your gift.

Beware of expressing appreciation of anything such as a tapestry or an embroidered cushion in your host's home, as it might then be given to you as a gift. Make sure you don't deprive your hosts of their valuable family heirlooms. Alternatively a similar item may be bought for you, which may be beyond people's means.

Usually, Pakistanis will give you a gift discreetly. Receive it with both hands. If it is wrapped, do not open it immediately. You can send your thanks later, and this will be appreciated. However, if it is not wrapped and presented in front of everyone, showing delight and appreciation will make your host satisfied.

DATING

As mentioned earlier, Pakistanis are generally conservative, and it is difficult for young people to meet the opposite sex without others making them feel uncomfortable. Internet and cell phones are frequently used by the young to chat and make friends. Usually, a young Pakistani woman meeting a foreigner will keep it secret to avoid unnecessary attention. Men, on the other hand, will show off, as having a foreigner for a friend (especially a fair-skinned woman) is seen as a trophy.

In the big cities there are clubs and art galleries where you can often meet new people. If you find a person who is eager to meet you privately, use your common sense. Meet in a restaurant or café rather than in a house or a hotel room. It is best not to give too much information about yourself or your movements to new acquaintances before you are confident enough to do so. If you will be staying away from your usual hotel or guest house to meet an acquaintance, it is advisable to inform someone locally—a friend, contact, or business partner—where you are going or how you can be reached.

chapter five

PRIVATE *&* FAMILY LIFE

Pakistan is a hierarchical society, in which people are respected because of their age and position. Forms of address are very important, and denote respect. The titles "Sahib" for a man and "Sahiba" for a woman are used by strangers as a sign of respect. Children are taught to address their elders using respectful titles, of which there are many, including "Uncle" and "Auntie." Only very close friends will call each other by their first names, and traditionally women do not address their husbands by name in public. The Western need for privacy is alien to Pakistani society in general, and people are curious to know what is going on around them. Talk of daily events is seized upon, repeated, and embroidered, and a story develops in no time.

HOUSING

Traditional Pakistani houses in rural areas are built with locally available material, such as mud mixed with straw, stones, and wood. Typically, each house consists of one or two big rooms with flat, thatched roofs, supported by a wooden pillar in the middle, and a walled courtyard where animals are tethered and where people sleep in the open in the hot summer. There are no windows, and one or two holes near the ceiling provide light and air. Some

houses have a veranda built out in front of the rooms to keep off the rain or heat. The kitchen is an open-air mud stove fueled by firewood or dried animal dung. Those who can afford it have a low thatched roof extending from the veranda or the main room over the kitchen. There will also be a *tanoor*, or *tanadoor* (clay oven) in a corner of the courtyard to bake bread, and a well. There are regional variations of communal facilities, such as mills and water collection, and communal use of ovens may be allowed by a baker, who will bake for a charge as well as selling bread. Toilets are nonexistent, and nearby fields are used for this purpose. Most rural houses are single story, but a pigeon house (dovecot) or storeroom may be built on the roof. In northern parts of the country, due to the harsh winter conditions, a large room is built on the rooftop, and is divided with wooden partitions into cooking and washing areas. Some villages have electricity, gas, and water pumps, and here the houses will have refrigerators, gas cookers, and other modern conveniences.

Traditional Pakistani houses in the cities are generally built in rows, facing a narrow lane, with three or four stories. Such a lane or street is known as a *mohallah*. The houses are built with mud bricks, using concrete for the flat roofs and flooring, though marble, stone, and mosaic work of marble chips are also used as flooring. The walls are usually plastered and painted with distemper or limestone. Wooden doors and windows are common, but iron gates have become a necessity for security reasons. These houses are multistory, and when a family expands, another story is added. Single family apartments are also being built in the main cities.

Rich, middle-class Pakistanis live in villas, locally known as *bangla* or *kothi*. These are usually double story, with large gardens at front and back, and with modern bathrooms and kitchens. Depending on the taste of the owner, you may see a mix of architectural styles in one house. Large French windows, Italian pillars, arches, and wooden panels are some of the features of these villas.

Pakistani feudal lords have huge houses, where they entertain the elite of the country. These are usually single story houses, built with some traditional features such as low arches, carved wooden panels, and ethnic décor, all the modern facilities, and a number of servants for maintenance. Outside are cattle sheds and chicken pens, surrounded by cultivated land.

The level of urbanization in Pakistan is the highest in South Asia. With the growing population, agricultural land is increasingly being used to build new houses in the rural areas. In some areas, villages near the cities have expanded and sprawled without planning, resulting in lack of local council services such as garbage collection or clean water supplies. As a result, slum and marginal human settlements, known as *kacchi abadi*, have spread in most urban localities. The growth of these informal settlements in the two megacities, Karachi and Lahore, has been particularly massive.

FAMILY LIVING

An average Pakistani family household consists of about eight people, probably including three or four children and grandparents. More affluent couples will have two or three children; poor or traditional rural dwellers will have more. Grandparents or unmarried uncles and aunts share the same house, and it is considered insane to live alone. A typical household is run by the women, who will start the day by preparing breakfast for everyone. Men and children will leave for work or school.

Traditionally, the roles are defined, and the senior man is the head of the family. He may or may not be the breadwinner, and could be a retired grandparent with authority. He may do the grocery shopping or other out-of-house tasks if women are unable or not allowed to do so. The average Pakistani man will not do any housework, such as washing dishes or cooking, and it is frowned upon if they do. Women do most of the housework, cleaning, laundry, and cooking, and sometimes the (female) children will be asked to help. It is interesting to note that in the cities more and more women are going out to work and are relying on mothers-in-law or other women in the household to look after the young children. Day-to-day decisions about what to cook, what to buy, and when, and who should be visited, are made by the women.

All city streets are busy in the mornings, with sellers of vegetables and other foods shouting at the tops of their lungs. Women call these vendors to their doorsteps and buy vegetables and other provisions for the day. Those who do not have vendors or live out of town do their daily shopping in the nearest corner shops, which sell basics for daily use. The word "bazaar" is used for a street of these shops, and a "market" is a bigger shopping

area of many shops and stalls. In some cities a few *mohallahs* will have a bazaar, and there are special shops for everything, with butchers, milk shops, a traditional bakery, and grocery stores.

RISHTAYDARI—KEEPING UP WITH RELATIVES

All Pakistanis belong to an extended family unit commonly known as *rishtaydari*—related through marriage. In a village everyone might be related to each other, as in an agriculture-based society people living in a small community used to depend on relatives for help, from the sowing of seeds to the harvest, and the family could be horizontal in many directions. By keeping social relations harmonious with these families, *rishtaydari* is kept alive. Usually, it is the women who keep up the connections and decide a visit is due. *Rishtaydari* could be also retributive—for example, if an uncle does not visit to congratulate a family when their son graduates, it will be remembered. Next time on a similar occasion the uncle will not only be ignored but an indirect message will be sent to remind him. Contributions toward a wedding are paid back accordingly, as an obligation, and if the payment is less than expected, this can result in bitterness. For a family celebration, the relatives are the first on the guest list, and friends are second. There is also a circle of close and less close relatives, and sometimes distant relatives become closer through another marriage.

If someone introduces you to a relative, don't ask him or her to explain the relationship, because it might be very confusing! The sister-in-law of a nephew could be as close to that person as a niece.

A maternal uncle is known as *mamoo* and his wife
will be *mamee*. A paternal uncle is *chacha* and his
wife is *chachee*. The maternal aunt is known as
khala and her husband is *khaloo*. The paternal
aunt is *phupi* and her husband is *phupa*.

Elder siblings will have their own titles, such as
lala, *bhaijan*, or *bhayya* for male siblings and *baji*,
booa, or *apa* for female. Wives of several brothers
have their own titles, and a daughter-in-law, son-in-
law, and grandchild from a daughter and from a son
have different names. In general, the wife of your
male friend is called by the title of *bhabi*. All these
titles are used in Urdu, and there are variations in
regional languages.

PRIVACY AND TABOOS

Most Pakistanis build their houses with a high
boundary wall to shield them from the gaze of
passersby. This applies to bungalows and Western-
style villas as well. In some cultures even the
apartment complexes are built in such a way that

balconies do not overlook the courtyards of neighbors. The word *chardiwari*, literally four walls, is used for the sanctity of a house. It is also used by religious zealots against women's emancipation. If a woman has the right to work outside the boundary of her home, such people consider this a violation of family life. Others argue that if she is confined to *chardiwari*, she is oppressed.

Family secrets such as sexual diseases, mental illnesses, and minor disabilities are taboos that everyone wants to avoid disclosing. Matters related to women are not discussed by men, but family conflicts are confided with close friends. Women are to be protected by the men of the family, and a brother must not be asked about his sister, as this would be considered shameful for both.

GROWING UP IN PAKISTAN

Most Pakistani children have siblings. Being an only child is very rare, and is often considered a privilege: *ladla* for a boy, or *ladlee* for a girl, means "the loved one." Children are hugged and kissed with affection, and usually sleep in their parents' beds until the age of five or six. They are expected to be obedient in manners and clever in studies. Sharing everything with siblings starts from the very beginning of their

lives. You will see children present at funerals, weddings, and parties, and they learn social skills from an early age.

A child's future depends on the economic situation of the parents, as education is not compulsory in Pakistan. Poor families have three options for their children's education. They can be admitted to government schools, separate for boys and girls, where education is free but classes are large, with poorly paid teachers. The second option for a boy is to learn a skill and become an apprentice at a young age. Girls will stay at home to be married off at puberty or when a suitable match is found. The third option for a boy is to be sent to a *madrassa*, or religious seminary, and study a set curriculum. The *madrassa* education is free; a boy can join at any age, and is allocated a course according to his ability. These schools are residential for orphans, who are provided with food and clothing, and many poor parents send a son to one to keep him out of trouble. There are some registered *madrassas* that include subjects like mathematics, social sciences, and languages. Since the 1980s, a large number of unregistered *madrassas*, financed by Middle Eastern donors, have been providing basic knowledge of religion, and some have turned into breeding grounds for terrorist organizations.

In a normal middle-class educated family both boys and girls start school at the age of five. They are expected to help with household chores; for example, a boy will be asked to buy groceries from a nearby shop and a girl will help her mother in housework after school. Children from these families are under a lot of pressure to obtain higher marks in exams, and some parents arrange special tuition for them in the evenings. Most professionals, such as doctors, engineers, civil servants, and military personnel, belong to this group. They send their children to English-medium schools, normally known as public schools. The upper classes, rich feudal families, and politicians educate their children in private schools based on the British public school system, which charge thousands of rupees in fees and have their own curricula. The elite Westernized class of Pakistanis comes from these schools.

Before the age of Nintendo and Wi-Fi, children would play in the streets after school and the neighborhood was usually considered safe. Now most children are busy with the latest gadgets and because of the security concerns of parents are not allowed to go out unaccompanied.

FURTHER EDUCATION

According to the Higher Education Commission of Pakistan there are 127 universities and institutes in the country. They produce about 445,000 graduates a year, with another 10,000 graduates of computer science. With the growth of the new wealthy middle and elite classes, private education at the college level is becoming more common. There are fifty-nine private universities supported by various bodies in different regions of the country. Khyber Pakhtoonkhwa Province has gained twenty more universities in the last ten years, and Balochistan has eight higher education institutes compared to one university in

1990. Despite these developments, Pakistan still has one of the lowest ratios in the world of people having access to higher education, the reason being the ever-increasing growth of the population and the divide between rich and poor.

LOVE AND MARRIAGE

Almost all folktales and poetry in Pakistan are based on passion and unfulfilled love. People love to tell, read, and write romantic stories, and most film and TV dramas are based on the true love of a boy and a girl. In real life, however, romance is taboo. In this conservative society, young people do not mix freely outside their own families and, as a result, cousins may flirt at family feasts and fall in love. If their parents find out, and if it's possible, a marriage between them is quickly arranged to avoid scandal.

Young Pakistani girls are still very traditional, and usually want marriage. Islamic traditions forbid a man to have a relationship with a girl if he does not intend to marry her. In most universities coeducation means that students do get to know each other, and love affairs develop. Young people are restrained from showing affection in public, and any illicit relationship is kept secret until there is a marriage prospect. Dating is therefore uncommon, and if a girl wants to meet a boy in a public place, she has to make an excuse to her family. In big cities like Karachi, Lahore, and Islamabad, some dare to break the rules, but in other, more conservative regions, meeting in public places is avoided.

In the twenty-first century the availability of cell phones and the Internet has opened the doors for young people to express themselves, and there is more romance through text messages and chats than in public places. A number of dating Web sites based in Pakistan allow the young, mostly men, to write about themselves and invite friendship. Women rarely advertise on these sites, and their electronic relationships develop privately.

MASHVARA AND NASEEHAT

An interesting aspect of traditional Pakistani society is the form of consultation called *mashvara*, and the giving of advice, or *naseehat*. There is usually a person in every village or extended family who is respected for his or her knowledge and experience of life. At a time of conflict, this figure may be approached for consultation. At a family level, there are aunts or uncles who have the authority to intervene to solve a problem. Some people take advantage of this position and give unsolicited advice on every matter, whether it is children's ailments, injuries, or business matters. Traditional medicinal cures for children, dealing with pests, and treatment for a sick donkey or hen are all part of the role. The parents of a naughty child or a wild youth might take him or her for *naseehat*—which usually means a lecture. This system, which provides support within the extended family, fulfills the role that is played by professional counseling or career guidance in the West.

chapter six

TIME OUT

The concept of going away on vacation does not exist in Pakistan, and during the long summer months, when the schools are closed, people stay at home or spend time with the extended family in villages if they have the option. People in business do not take breaks, apart from weekends. As most small businesses are run by one person, staying away from work would incur a loss of earnings. For most people a popular form of recreation is visiting family and friends for a special meal. Those with low incomes will relax at weddings, where everyone enjoys the feast with music and dancing.

Men and women are segregated in public places, though families will be seen together, shopping, eating, or going for a walk. Other entertainment is very much divided between the genders. Men in the outside world have access to physical activities, such as sports, and to cinemas, restaurants, and clubs. Women normally stay at home, watch TV dramas, cook elaborate meals, or go shopping. A favorite pastime for the average Pakistani is watching big sports events, like football, cricket, and hockey, on TV. There are popular places with historical monuments and nature resorts where students may go on day excursions arranged by their schools or colleges. Picnics are not very common, except in springtime when the weather is tolerable.

EATING OUT

The traditional outdoor eating places in Pakistan evolved from teahouses (*chaikhana*), where there was a samovar of hot water for a refreshing cup of tea and food for travelers. Hotels offering food were built in the big cities in the twentieth century, and therefore Pakistanis refer to a restaurant as a "hotel." In some cultures eating outside was only for travelers, and traditionally it was out of necessity rather than pleasure. Today roadside eateries selling *kababs* (barbecued meat) or *dal-roti* (lentils and bread) from a clay oven, with low-level seats for you to sit on, are still popular and economical places for a meal out. They may not be the best venues, but they provide simple, freshly prepared food of the region. Eating in a restaurant is becoming more fashionable, and young people will dress up to go out and eat a burger as a special treat.

In a typical Pakistani restaurant you can find meat, vegetable curries, and lentils served with bread and soft drinks. There are no single portions, and the food is served in bowls to share. Normally, the

waiter, known as a *beraa*, will tell you how big a portion is. You choose from the menu, and sometimes the dish can be customized to your taste. Beware of the word "hot," especially in Punjab and Sindh. If you ask for mild food, there will still be chilies in it, which you might find very hot—so say "no chilies" when ordering, if this is what you want. Bland food is considered fit only for an ill person.

In an ordinary restaurant, you will find plastic or stainless steel plates, with a tablespoon for eating rice. Pakistanis are great bread eaters, and break off a small piece by hand to scoop up curries and beans from their plate. Most good restaurants are air-conditioned and look clean, but observe the cloth used to wipe the tables and that will give you some idea of the standard of hygiene. (More on this in Chapter 7.)

FOOD AND DRINK

Within Pakistan the cuisine varies greatly from region to region, reflecting the country's ethnic and cultural diversity. Food from Punjab and Sindh is quite similar to the cuisine of northern India, and can be highly seasoned and spicy. In other parts of the country, particularly in the north and west, mild, aromatic spices are used in cooking, and less oil. Pakistanis are meat eaters, and although there are all sorts of seasonal vegetables and fruits available, you will find very few vegetarian options in the restaurants. Given the diversity of cultures, cuisines generally differ from home to home, and may be totally different from the standard Pakistani fare of curry and bread.

Muslims are forbidden to eat pork or drink alcohol, and *halal* dietary guidelines are strictly observed. Beef (both cow and buffalo meat), lamb, and chicken are available everywhere, and curried meat is the staple diet of most people. In certain parts of Punjab, beef is not liked, and goat's meat is preferred. Lentils are considered poor people's food in other cultures. Salad is usually onions, tomatoes, cucumber, and green chilies with lemon. Chutney is green coriander or

mint pounded in a pestle and mortar, mixed with crushed green chilies, garlic, tomatoes, or yogurt. Pickles have a sharp, pungent taste and contain many spices and salt as preservatives. The idea of cooking frozen vegetables is alien to the majority of the population, as frozen food is expensive and most people cannot afford it.

International cuisine and fast food are popular in the cities. Blending local and foreign recipes, or fusion food, such as burger *kababs* or Pakistani Chinese, is common in the large urban centers.

Street stalls sell a variety of snacks, such as chickpeas with onion and spices known as *cholay*, gram flour vindaloo in yogurt sauce, *dahi barre*, *pakora, and samosa.* In summer the yogurt drink *lassi*, a variety of ice creams, *kulfi*, and an iced sugar drink known as *sherbat* are sold in most streets.

Famous Baloch and Pashtun dishes, such as lamb-skewered *sajji* and *chapli kabab*, have gained massive popularity in different parts of Pakistan.

Dampukht is meat cooked in steam, and *khaddi kabab*, a whole lamb or goat stuffed with rice, is cooked on a spit over an open fire. For an authentic taste of Pakistan, try a creamy *korma*, a savory *aab gosht* curry, marinated boneless chicken *tikka*, and freshly baked bread.

Sindh is home to a large Hindu population, and interesting vegetarian dishes with lentils and beans can be tasted in the streets. The area is also famous for pickles and chutneys. In the northwest, the influence of Afghan food such as *Kabuli pullao* and various *kababs* can be experienced. Food in Islamabad and other tourist resorts is not restricted to traditional Pakistani dishes, as fast-food chains are rising in popularity due to their convenience and family-oriented style.

Bread

Pakistanis are great bread eaters, and you will find many varieties throughout the country, from freshly baked hot *naans* to the thin disks of *chappatis*. Each region has its own characteristic kind of bread. Clay-oven baked bread has two variations: Punjabi bread, which is unleavened, and the other, *naan*, which has yeast in it and is eaten mostly in Pashtun and Baloch areas. *Naan* can be

stuffed with minced mutton (*qeema naan*), or sweetened with syrup (*shirmaal*), and there is oily *roghani naan* for breakfast. In Sindh and Punjab thin flat bread (*chapatti*) is made without yeast; in other areas it has yeast mixed in the dough. A "bakery" in Pakistan sells Western-style bread. Known as "*double roti*," this is usually white, and it is also available in most general stores. These bakeries also make cookies, cakes, and pastries, and you will be surprised to find localized pizzas, buns, and even baguettes. Whole wheat sliced bread is scarce; you will find it in some bakeries, but make sure it is whole wheat, and not just brown-colored bread.

Drinks

Chai (tea) is popular throughout the country. It is black tea, brewed with milk and sugar. Almost all Pakistanis have this thick tea for breakfast with bread. You will be offered tea when visiting a house, or in shops and offices where workers will take tea breaks between the meals. Afternoon tea in Pakistan is a legacy of the Raj, and is usually accompanied by cookies, cakes, or *samosas*.

In Khyber Pakhtunkhwa and Balochistan, green tea with cardamom, known as *kahva* or *sabz chai*, is popular, and you can have it, with or without sugar, all day long. Lemon is optional, but is recommended with green tea. Kashmiri *chai* is a special green tea brewed for a long time with cardamom, and when the milk is added it becomes pink. It is creamy, can be sweet or salty, and may have almonds and nuts added to give additional flavor. This tea is very popular at wedding feasts and in the cold season.

In the warmer southern region, sweet drinks are readily available throughout the day. Look for street vendors who have fruits (real or decorative) hanging from their roofs. Some milk/yogurt shops serve *lassi*, which can be sweet or salty, or the rich, thick variety with mango pulp, known as "mango *lassi*." Fizzy drinks like Coke, Pepsi, Fanta, and Sprite are sold in bottles and in some areas, instead of referring to them by name, the word "bottle" is used, meaning a fizzy soft drink. Don't confuse this with an alcoholic drink if you are asked to have a "bottle."

Alcohol (both imported and local) is available to non-Muslim foreigners at liquor stores and at bars in most top hotels. The local alcoholic beer is called Murree Beer. It is illegal for Muslims to buy, possess, or consume alcohol, but there is a huge black market across the country, and the police tend to turn a blind eye to what goes on in private. Alcohol is also easily available in high-class restaurants and clubs.

SPORTS AND GAMES

Field hockey is the national game of Pakistan, and is the sport in which it has been most successful at the Olympics, with three gold medals. It has won the Hockey World Cup four times. Pakistan was a dominant player of squash for many decades, winning the World Open seventeen times and the British Open twelve times. But, if you ask a Pakistani youth about his or her favorite game, it will, without a doubt, be cricket.

There are thousands of local cricket clubs and even in the villages children play cricket from an early age. No other game unifies Pakistanis like cricket, and large numbers of people gather around TV sets to watch the national team play in world competitions, especially in matches against India. Occasionally the government announces a day off for a final, and it is celebrated as a festival.

Recently, football (soccer) has grown in popularity across the country, and the Fédération Internationale de Football Association (FIFA) has teamed up with the government to bring it closer to the northern areas. Other popular sports are volleyball, netball (basketball), tennis, and table tennis.

Polo is important in northern Pakistan, with major competitions in the spring and summer months. Pakistan is one of only eight nations to play polo professionally, and fields some twenty-six professional clubs. The most famous club is Lahore Polo Club, in which the facilities are first-rate; foreign teams often play there in friendly games.

Kite flying is a favorite pastime of the youth all year-round. *Kabbadi* and *kushti* are some of the indigenous forms of wrestling. Bodybuilding clubs are popular among the young, and local clubs arrange competitions.

Pakistan has hosted several international competitions, including the South Asian Federation Games—multisport competitions in which eight regional countries of South Asia participate.

The Tour de Pakistan, modeled on the Tour de France, is an annual cycling competition that covers the length and breadth of the country. Starting in Karachi and ending in Peshawar, a distance of 1,024 miles (1,648 km), it is the longest and one of the most difficult cycling races in Asia.

CULTURAL ACTIVITIES

Pakistan is home to two unique schools of art: the Moghul Miniature genre, which has no match in the world; and the syncretic twentieth-century revivalist Chughtai style, of which the painters Abdul Rahman Chughtai and Allah Bakhsh are the most famous exponents.

The Pakistani love of color is seen in everyday life, in the brightly colored painted houses, doors, and windows. On the roads exuberantly decorated trucks and buses, painted with mountain scenery, religious calligraphy, or verses from the famous regional poets, are ubiquitous.

Formal arts and cultural activities are confined to the big cities, and there are Arts Councils in all the provincial capitals that organize theater festivals and arts exhibitions. Going to the theater and concerts is still the preserve of the elite and of city dwellers.

Pakistanis love poetry and drama, which have evolved from the oral traditions of storytelling. Storytelling and poetry, which is sometimes sung, still exist in some form in rural areas and can be experienced at weddings and other local celebrations. Because there is no homogeneous culture, the arts are different in every region.

Pakistani music embraces wide variety of genres, ranging from classical styles such as *qawwali* and *ghazal* to more modern forms that fuse traditional Pakistani music with Western music. Nusrat Fateh Ali Khan was internationally renowned for blending *qawwali* with Western music.

The most notable popular forms of music are film music and Urdu and regional pop music. There are also the diverse traditions of folk music, as well as modern styles.

Dancing accompanies many events, such as weddings and other festivities. Male group dances reflect the agricultural and warrior traditions of the people. The drum, the lute, and the shepherd's flute are the most common instruments accompanying the singing and dancing. Popular folk dances include Punjabi *bhangra*, *sammi*, *luddi*, *giddha*, and *kikly*, Sindhi *ho-jamalo*, *dhamal*, and *jhumar*, Pashtun *attan* (also known as *khattak*), and Balochi *lewa*.

Pakistan's indigenous movie industry, known as Lollywood, produces more than forty feature-length films a year. It flourished in the 1960s, with Lahore as its hub, but it dwindled during the Islamization of Zia-ul-Haq in the 1980s. Pakistan Television dramas are more popular than films and, with satellite and cable channels, Indian soaps have a large viewing in the country. Pakistanis are also fond of Indian films, which officially are not allowed to be shown in cinemas, though recently the government has relaxed this ban. Western movies are heavily censored before they are screened, and all kissing and sexual content are removed by the censor board.

Unfortunately, the Afghan war, the influx of insurgents, and the ongoing conflict have affected cultural activities in Balochistan and Khyber Pakhtunkhwa. Musicians and singers were under threat from Islamists, especially in the Pashtun areas. With the killing of local singers, artists have been forced to flee to other cities or leave the country.

SHOPPING FOR PLEASURE

The average Pakistani city dweller shops daily for food, but shopping for clothes, shoes, and other luxury items is a hobby for many middle- and upper-class women, and tourists consider the country a shopping paradise. In the past three decades, returning migrants working in the Gulf have invested money in property and businesses. As a result, new shopping malls have mushroomed all over the country, selling goods from the Far East, central Asia, and Europe. On the other hand, the atmospheric old bazaars in the cities of Lahore and Peshawar have the same tiny alleys, some of which will just admit a rickshaw or a cart, with pedestrians having to leap into doorways to make room.

You have to go to the right market or shopping area for a specific item. There is no standard price setting, and bargaining is common. Pakistani shopkeepers are excellent salesmen, and they are very friendly to foreigners. If a shop is not busy when you walk in, the salesman will happily show you his merchandise and serve you tea or cold drinks, even if you tell him that you are only comparing prices. Sometimes there is no agreement on price, and it is still perfectly acceptable

to leave the shop without buying anything. For the best market price you will have to shop around, but if you are pressed for time you could go to the big, Western-style shopping centers, exclusive boutiques, and specialty shops, which have price tags.

Pakistani textiles are among the best in the world, and the mills in Punjab produce cotton fabrics for dressmaking, scarves, and bed linen that compete in the international market. Faisalabad has one of the largest textile industries in the world, and many internationally renowned brands have their products prepared by the mills of this city. The city of Sialkot in Punjab produces 90 percent of the world's sports goods, and is the largest provider of sports equipment to FIFA for the World Cup. It is also famous for some of the finest surgical instruments, and leather goods such as shoes, jackets, and bags. Wood carving, decorative green marble items, jewelry, glass and crystal ware, brassware, antiques, gem craft, pottery, and pashmina shawls are some of the favorite items for tourists.

Apart from Pakistani products, you can also buy Chinese-made goods, especially electronic items, and Afghan carpets.

SIGHTSEEING

Six major cultural sites in Pakistan are listed as UNESCO World Heritage Sites. These include the archaeological ruins at Mohenjodaro and the

monuments of the ancient city of Thatta in Sindh; the first-century Buddhist monastery at Takht Bahai and at Siribahlol in Khyber Pakhtunkhwa; Rohtas fort at Jhelum; the ruins of Taxila; the Lahore Fort; and the Shalimar Gardens in Punjab. In 2009, the World Economic Forum's Travel and Tourism Competitiveness Report ranked Pakistan

as one of the top 25 percent tourist destinations for its World Heritage Sites.

Pakistan has twenty-seven public and private museums and ten art galleries, the largest number of which are in Punjab. The city of Lahore, with its many buildings of Mughal architecture, must not be missed.

The mountain ranges attract adventurers and mountaineers from around the world—especially K2, the second-highest peak in the world, after Mount Everest. The northern hill stations are favorite venues for spring and winter sports, and the romance of the historic Khyber Pass is timeless.

chapter seven

TRAVEL, HEALTH, & SAFETY

The international profile of Pakistan may discourage visitors. The western border areas are notorious for militancy, and government forces are struggling to keep the conflict under control. However, the country is visited by thousands of Europeans and other nationals every year, both on business and as tourists, and there are agencies that work to attract tourism and take measures for security as well. When you arrive at an international airport in Pakistan you may see a heavy police presence, but this should be reassuring rather than threatening.

There are no restrictions on the amount of foreign currency you are allowed to bring in, and money can be changed anywhere. If you have a cell phone with a roaming facility, you will immediately get a message from the local server (usually Mobilink) and your phone will be active. You can buy a SIM card with a local number, even at the airport, with top-up facilities. Pakistan has the latest electronic communications links with the rest of the world, and you will be surprised to find the most modern gadgets even in a corner shop.

If you visit between April and September, be prepared for extreme heat, and wear cotton clothing and a hat, sunglasses, and sandals. The winter months are mild in the south, but the northern parts are cold, with temperatures dropping below the freezing point in the mountains. People tend to be impatient in public places, and complaining loudly is normal behavior. Everywhere you go are the sounds of power generators and the smell of burning diesel, due to the constant problems of electricity breakdown and rolling blackouts.

VISAS

Almost all nationalities require a visa to visit Pakistan. This is usually easier to obtain in your home country. Tourist visas are normally issued on the same day, but business visas take five working days to process. For a business visa, applicants are required to have a letter of invitation from Pakistan, and visas are now issued for up to five years. Those working for a nongovernment organization need to provide proof of registration with the Economic Affairs Division (EAD) in Pakistan or with the Interior Ministry. Foreign companies based in Pakistan are asked to provide their registration proof with the application form.

Recently a list of twenty-four "Tourist Friendly Countries" (TFC) was announced, whose nationals are eligible for one-month visas on arrival if they travel through an authorized tour operator who will assume responsibility for them while they're in the country. Nationals of a handful of countries are issued visas on arrival for one month. Check the Web site of the Pakistani High Commission or embassy in your own country.

Nationals of Israel are not allowed entry because it is not recognized as a state by Pakistan, but there is no restriction on Jews holding passports from other countries. Despite much online information to the contrary, Israeli stamps and visas do not usually pose problems for entry into Pakistan, though you may be subject to more stringent questioning by immigration officers.

Indian nationals can apply for thirty-day tourist visas but must travel in a group through an authorized tour operator. Visitor visas to meet relatives or friends are easier to obtain, and come with some restrictions. To visit the religious shrines, visas are granted for groups of ten or more for fifteen days.

Nationals of Afghanistan are refused entry if their passports or tickets show evidence of transit or boarding in India. Holders of Taiwanese passports are refused entry except for airport transit.

ARRIVAL

By Air

Pakistan has forty-eight airports—ten for international travel and others for local flights. Karachi, Lahore, Peshawar, Quetta, and Islamabad are the main ports for most international flights. Karachi and Lahore are the best at dealing with luggage and immigration. Islamabad is a shambles, and is waiting to be moved to a brand-new building near Fateh Jang. Peshawar has flights coming from the Gulf States and Saudi Arabia, and is used mostly by the migrant workers in these countries. Pakistan International Airlines flies to several countries and has a good reputation, but it can be very busy even in off-peak times. There are two private airlines for internal flights, Air Blue and Shaheen, which also compete with the big airlines on some international flights.

Foreigners usually pass quickly through immigration and passport control, but at some airports you have a long wait to collect your baggage. Pakistanis tend to travel with a lot of bags and grab more than one trolley, which can create a shortage for other passengers and porters. If you ask one of the porters, though, you will get one sooner, with their service as well. The porters' fee is fixed, and if you are a woman on your own they will get your bags off the conveyer belt, put them on the trolley, and even wait while you pass through customs. Some airports scan your boxes again, which can be annoying, but security-conscious Pakistanis don't want to take any chances.

Outside you will be met with noisy crowds waiting for their loved ones, and with taxi drivers asking for your destination. Don't expect anyone in a kiosk marked "Information" to provide you with much useful service. Your porter may have more information—if he can speak your language.

By Land

Although Pakistan shares land borders with four countries, crossing any of these by road is precarious and subject to the current political situation. The Grand Trunk Road (GT Road) is one of South Asia's oldest and longest major roads. For several centuries, it has linked the eastern and western regions of South Asia, running from Bengal in the east across north India to Pakistan, and across Punjab to the northwest of the country.

From India, two train services operate: the Samjhota Express from Delhi to Lahore, and the Thar Express from Jodhpur to Karachi. There is an international bus service between Delhi and Lahore that is just as fast, much more flexible, and much cheaper than the train.

Coming from China, the Karakoram Highway, the highest paved international road in the world, makes its way from Kashgar in Xinjiang Province through the Khunjerab Pass to Abbottabad, in Pakistan.

Pakistan has train links with Iran, though this is not the fastest or most practical way to enter the country. There is a broad-gauge railway line running from Zahedan in southeastern Iran to Quetta on the western edge of Pakistan; a standard-gauge line from Zahedan to Kirman in central Iran links it with the rest of the Iranian rail network. This train journey, through spectacular mountain scenery, is an experience in its own right. If speed is a priority it is best to take the bus via the Mijva border area in Iran, half an hour's drive from Zahedan. The corresponding Pakistani border town, Taftan, has immigration and customs facilities.

From Afghanistan there are two official border crossings: one in Torkham, through the Khyber Pass, and the other in Chaman, near Quetta. On each side of the border there is an immigration post in which your passport, which must have a valid visa, is stamped. To come through the Khyber Pass you will need special permission from the Commissioner's Office in Peshawar, which will provide you with an armed escort through the tribal areas for safety. The Bolan Pass connects Quetta to Kandahar in Afghanistan, and is considered very dangerous. This route is currently closed to foreign tourists, and is only open to locals and aid workers. Although there are two official check posts and border crossings with Afghanistan, the long border is porous and is crossed illegally by Pashtun tribes, who do not recognize it.

GETTING AROUND
By Air
Pakistan International Airlines (PIA), serves thirty-eight domestic airports, with scheduled daily flights between all the main cities. There are also private airlines, Shaheen and Air Blue, serving Karachi, Lahore, Faisalabad, and Islamabad. Fares are not cheap, so most people travel by other means. Daily flights leave Islamabad for the northern tourist regions of Gilgit, Skardu, and Saidu Sharif, and there is a weekly air safari over the northern mountains that leaves every Saturday, also from Islamabad. Daily flights from Peshawar to Chitral are subject to the weather conditions.

By Road

Thousands of Pakistanis travel by road between cities every day. This is the cheapest and most reliable mode of transportation. The construction of freeways began in the early 1990s with the idea of building a world-class road network and to reduce the load on the heavily used national highways throughout the country. The M2 was the first freeway, completed in 1998, linking the cities of Islamabad and Lahore. In the past five years many new freeways have opened up, connecting north and south. The maintenance of old roads, however, has not been as efficient as expected, and most small villages in Pakistan have dirt tracks that are dusty in dry weather and muddy when it rains.

The "Silk Road" is an extensive interconnected network of the old trade routes across the Asian continent, connecting east, south, and western Asia with the rest of the world. Following the Karakoram Highway, it passes through the middle of Pakistan, through the cities of Peshawar, Taxila, and Multan. Private buses and "wagons" (minibuses) carry passengers from one end to the other.

There are more motorcycles than any other vehicles on Pakistani roads. Over the years, however, the number of cars on Pakistani roads has tripled, and traffic jams are a common sight in major cities.

Traditional Modes of Travel

Traditional modes of travel are still common in the small towns of Pakistan, where people walk great distances to get to work or do their daily shopping. The donkey cart, locally known as the *rairhi*, is still visible everywhere, as the poor use this form of transportation for moving loads, ranging from fruits and vegetables to textiles or even machinery for factories in the industrial cities. The horse and carriage, locally known as a *tanga*, is mainly used

for casual traveling around the city. There is one driver, and one horse. The *tanga* is a favorite with spring and summer tourists, who love to see the cities from an open vehicle. Camels and camel-drawn carts are also seen in the hotter parts of Pakistan, including Sindh, Punjab, and Balochistan, where farmers transport larger loads that donkey carts cannot manage. Bicycles are used by the poor, office workers, and schoolboys.

Buses

Local bus services in the big cities are run by both the local authorities and private companies. Fares on the public services are cheaper. Destinations are marked on the front or side of the bus. In some cities there are minibuses, known as "wagons," which stop on request if they have enough room. Their stops are not marked, and you have to guess at these from the crowds waiting by the roadside.

There are several private coach companies offering good intercity services. One of the best is the Sammi Daewoo Express, which has air-

conditioned coaches serving all the main cities and many others, with shuttle services from the coaches to local neighborhoods. Tickets are booked in advance, and payment is made at the bus station before the journey.

Other well-established intercity bus services are Kohistan, Khan Brothers, Skyways, and Niazi Express, which run twenty-four hours a day. Buses leave the major bus stations for big cities and many smaller locations every few minutes, so booking ahead is neither possible nor necessary. Fares are often (though not always) paid directly on the bus.

There is sometimes very little knee space on these buses, and no air-conditioning, but you'll get to your destination. There is usually a conductor who has several duties on the journey, such as signaling to the driver to start or stop by banging on the side of the bus, closing the door, collecting the fares, and giving information to passengers. The conductors are usually friendly and helpful. There will probably be loud piped music, controlled by the driver from his seat, usually consisting of songs from Pakistani or Indian movies. It won't be turned down, even if a passenger complains. The drivers are free spirits, and if one spots a friend driving another bus there is likely to be a race and an exchange of greetings or insults, to the dismay of the passengers. If you experience this, just close your eyes and pray for a police car or traffic jam to end the adventure.

Rickshaws and Taxis

The ubiquitous auto-rickshaw is the most common form of transportation for short distances. It is small enough to squeeze through a traffic jam by getting into gaps between slow-moving traffic, passing bigger vehicles on the left or right, and sometimes driving with a wheel on the footpath—scaring pedestrians out of the way—to speed up the journey. These diesel- and liquid gas-run vehicles are noisy, bumpy, uncomfortable, and more exposed to the weather than a taxi. For some people they can be more fun, however, and if you have to use one, make sure you negotiate the fare beforehand with the driver. Auto-rickshaws in Pakistan do not generally have meters, or anyway reliable ones. Rickshaws are banned in the capital, Islamabad, because of their noise.

A new form of short-distance vehicle in Pakistan is the *qing-qi* (pronounced "chin-chi"), which is a cross between a motorcycle and an auto-rickshaw. These run just like a motorcycle, but have

three wheels instead of two. They can carry a heavier load and have a greater capacity than an auto-rickshaw. They sometimes follow set routes, and carry multiple passengers.

There are yellow cabs (taxis), which can be hired directly from airports and hotels. It is also possible to order a radio car by phone, either individually or from the cab company office. The service is currently offered in Islamabad, Rawalpindi, Karachi, Lahore, and Peshawar. Drivers charge according to a meter usually located on the dashboard, but fares can be negotiated if there is no meter. Foreigners are routinely charged double for everything, so ask a local person in advance how much the fare should be. Don't get into a cab before ensuring that the driver knows where to go, or before negotiating the price. Don't be afraid to bargain. When you have agreed on the fare and climbed in, prepare the exact sum you'll be paying; no tips are required.

Driving

If you are not scared off by the unruly traffic conditions, you can get a local driving license very easily, and you will get used to the system within a few days. You drive on the left side of the road, because of Pakistan's former British colonial status.

You will see the traffic police on main traffic circles, but they can't control everything, especially during the rush hours, and some people think that driving in Pakistan is like purposely courting death. Even if there are demarcated lanes, people don't stay in them, happily passing other cars while breaking the speed limit. Honking the horns is normal behavior.

There are a couple of road journeys in particular that visitors like to take for sightseeing. One is the

route on the Karakoram Highway from Islamabad up to the northern mountains, and the other is the Makran Coastal Highway between Karachi and the port of Gwadar, in Balochistan.

Trains

Pakistan Railways is a state-run passenger and cargo service under the supervision of the Ministry of Railways. The trains carry sixty-five million passengers annually, and daily operate 228 mail, express, and passenger services. There are several different classes of fare, depending on amenities. Foreign tourists and students can get 25 percent and 50 percent discounts respectively by first getting a verification certificate from the Pakistan Tourism Development Corporation (PTDC) office and bringing it with them to the train's commercial ticket office; this is not the regular ticket office, but is usually close by. Pakistan Railways boasts about first-class carriages, but they do not provide a good service. It is precarious, and may not have all the

modern facilities of air-conditioning and running water. Rail journeys in Pakistan are an experience of a lifetime, still much as described in Rudyard Kipling's *Kim*. The crowded stations have noisy vendors selling all sorts of food and soft drinks. The slow-moving trains have separate carriages for men and women. The seats—just wooden benches—are uncomfortable for long journeys. Vendors hop on and off the trains, and the passengers talk to each other throughout the journey. If you just want to try the trains, take one for a short journey during the daytime.

A new service for businesses has opened from Rawalpindi to Karachi, connecting other major cities on the way. But it is facing crises of fuel shortage and revenue deficit, and a move for the privatization of the railway is still being debated.

WHERE TO STAY

There are, of course, five-star international hotels with good facilities and high standards. Aside from these, foreign tourists are often disappointed by the cleanliness, or lack of cleanliness, that they find in Pakistan's hotels. The bedding is usually clean, but bathrooms can be grungy. Ask to see the room first, and check the beds, toilets, lights, and so on before checking in. Bargaining for a good rate is common.

The government-run PTDC hotels fall into the middle of the range, and are often the oldest in the town. Such places will have air-conditioning and hot water, but may not have a generator to operate these facilities during electricity down times. The cheapest hotels are found around busy transportation hubs.

Guesthouses, which are popular and often cheaper than hotels, might be conventional apartments or private homes in the more affluent parts of town. They are usually run as a private business, with staff who might leave in the evenings. If you are concerned about your safety, a well-recommended place with its own guard might be a better option. Corporations and government agencies may have their own guesthouses.

HEALTH

The summer months are very hot in Pakistan, except in the mountains. You need to keep hydrated, and sealed bottled water or soft drinks and tea are the safest way. Some innocent-looking drinks, such as freshly squeezed orange or carrot juice, can be lethal if the juice extractor has not been properly cleaned, and budget places sometimes offer free filtered water, but even that is dubious. You are strongly advised not to drink tap water, which is known to contain impurities. Ice is usually made from regular tap water, and should be avoided. Fresh milk from the carrier should be boiled and cooled before consumption. Milk cartons (known as "milk packs") are trusted, and are available at most grocery stores, but check the labels for expiration dates.

Food hygiene can be precarious, and it is wise to assess this carefully, because diarrhea is one of the commonest illnesses that visitors experience. Some Pakistani curries and snacks can be very hot and spicy, which can cause an upset stomach. Always notify your host, cook, or waiter if you cannot take very spicy food. Don't eat food that has been lying about for some time in a warm room, as this speeds up deterioration. Also, be very careful where you eat. Avoid an unfrequented restaurant even if it looks all right, because if it is not good enough for Pakistanis it is not good enough for you. Also avoid eating cooked food from markets or roadside stands if they do not look clean.

With the constant rolling blackouts of electricity, refrigeration of food can be badly affected. Meat or poultry that has not been kept properly frozen is one of the main causes of diarrhea. Apart from the big hotels, where power generators keep the flow of electricity constant, kitchens in other places may not be safe, or clean. Meat that is barbecued in front of you may be all right, but if you are in doubt, avoid it.

Generally the most populated areas of Pakistan have a problem of waste disposal, with open sewers breeding mosquitoes. Take precautions against malaria, which is common between April and October except in areas above 6,500 feet (2,000 m). Ensure your accommodation is mosquito proof, and take measures to avoid bites by using an insect repellent and wearing long, loose-fitting, light-colored clothing.

Dengue, also known as breakbone fever, is caused by a virus from the dengue mosquito, and can only be prevented with precautionary measures, as there is no vaccination or specific treatment available for it.

Although yellow fever is not a risk in Pakistan, the government requires travelers arriving from countries where the disease exists to present proof of vaccination, and it is wise to check this at the time of your visa application.

Medical Treatment

There are a number of good private clinics and hospitals in the major cities. For common ailments anywhere in the country you can visit a general practitioner and pay a fee for a consultation and prescription. It is possible to buy medicines without a prescription, but make sure that you get them from a reputable pharmacy. The private clinics and hospitals usually require up-front payment, confirmation of insurance coverage, or guarantee of payment prior to admission.

Medical treatment in government hospitals is free, but you have to wait in line to see the consultant in an outpatient department (OPD), and the standard of facilities and care is generally limited.

SAFETY

Pakistan is one of the most dangerous countries in the world, and is, of course, a neighbor of Afghanistan. There is a lot of confusion in the West about the safety of Western travelers, but the situation in Pakistan is entirely different from that in Iraq and Afghanistan and for the ordinary traveler it's a generally hospitable country.

Before traveling you should check with your embassy about off-limits areas and the latest political and military developments, and keep a close eye on current issues with independent news sources. Acts of terrorism are of serious concern, and extremist groups have been known to target American and Western interests in certain areas of the country. Demonstrations aren't uncommon, and should be avoided at all costs. In early 2006, the Prophet Mohammad cartoon protests quickly got out of hand, and several businesses were torched, along with scores of cars. If a large demonstration or protest is under way, try to avoid it. Use common sense when hanging out with friends, and definitely avoid being intoxicated in public in this Islamic country.

Familiarize yourself with the Urdu words for yes (*han*), no (*nahin*), left (*baaen*), right (*daaen*), forward (*seedha*), and stop (*rukko*), write them down, and keep them with you. Sometimes visitors try Arabic, thinking that people will speak it in an Islamic country, but, apart from the greetings and *Alhamdulillah* (praise to God), Pakistanis do not speak or understand it.

You may see road signs in English saying "No foreigners allowed beyond this point," for example, on the road to Kahuta near Islamabad, which is the nuclear base. If you want to pass one of these signs, turn back and find another route, or stop at the nearest police station and see if they will let you pass. Typical restricted areas are those with military installations nearby. Being caught in one will mean a lot of wasted time, embarrassment, and the possible involvement of your embassy. Try to be as inconspicuous as possible and do not make yourself obvious as a tourist.

Women traveling through Pakistan should adopt local dress customs and avoid traveling alone, especially at night. Although US nationals are advised not to use public transportation in Pakistan, safety will mainly depend on the current situation. Many foreign visitors do use public transportation, with local advice, and you can do the same. Take up-to-date recommendations from a reliable source.

The best safety tip for business travelers is to have a local cell phone and input the numbers of the people you are going to meet. Then if you (or your driver) are lost, call up the person you are meeting and ask for directions.

In general, visitors will find the locals very curious, and very eager to help. Being friendly and smiling at people goes a long way. If you're a woman, though, it's best to be sparing with your smiles, lest people get too friendly. This is more likely to happen in areas such as bazaars or on public transportation than anywhere else.

EMERGENCY NUMBERS

Police Help Line 15

Rescue Services 1122

English is spoken on these lines in the major cities.

Finally, a word of reassurance. It is worth remembering that significant trading deals and investment projects are carried out successfully even in the troubled areas, thanks to the secure and well-established infrastructure with its railway, bus, and postal services.

culture smart! **pakistan**

BUSINESS BRIEFING

The World Bank and International Finance Corporation's flagship report *Ease of Doing Business Index 2010* ranked Pakistan eighty-fifth of 181 countries around the globe—the highest in South Asia. Even in the context of all the troubles the country is facing, it is considered a good place for investment, according to *Forbes Magazine* in 2011. There are challenges, of course, but it has a large and growing domestic market, a growing middle class, and a well-established infrastructure. It is a principal gateway to Central Asia, and has connections with the Middle East and South Asia.

In recent years the uncertain political situation and better job opportunities abroad have led many Pakistanis to seek work outside the country. The flight of qualified doctors, engineers, and scientists is a cause for concern. Highly skilled businesspeople, however, are thriving locally. The low-skilled  laborers who leave to work in the Gulf are quickly replaced by others, who play their role in the local economy. Surprisingly, there are seven Chambers of Commerce and Industry for women throughout Pakistan, which help to promote women-run businesses.

That Pakistan is home to more than six hundred foreign companies demonstrates its liberal economic policy. There are few restrictions on holding foreign currency, or on bringing it in or out of the country. There are no limits on the inflow or outflow of funds for remittances of profits, debt service, capital gains, returns on intellectual property, or payments for imported goods. The infrastructure includes comprehensive road, rail, and sea links; good-quality telecommunications and IT services; modern company laws; and a long-standing corporate culture. The telecommunications industry has grown fourteenfold since 2000; Pakistan has ninety-one million people plugged into its mobile networks, with one of the highest mobile teledensities in the world. With a high economic growth rate in recent years, Pakistan is developing rapidly, and the number of business opportunities is increasing.

BUSINESS CULTURE

Pakistan's business culture is strongly group oriented. Individual preferences are less important than the sense of belonging to a group and conforming to its norms. Business relationships here exist between people, not necessarily between companies. Therefore it is important to be introduced by a trusted third party when approaching prospective partners. Even when you have their friendship and trust, they will not necessarily trust others from your company. That makes it very important to keep your company contacts unchanged.

Pakistan is entrepreneurial to the core, with cheap raw materials and a motivated workforce. Small businesses thrive in the back streets of big cities, and sometimes a whole community will be engaged in the production process in one particular area. The business community is known to be hardworking, and it is common for some businesses to be open seven days a week. Because Pakistanis prefer to work with people they know and trust, they will spend a great deal of time on the getting-to-know-you part of relationship building. What in the West would be considered nepotism is viewed positively, since it guarantees hiring people who can be trusted, which is crucial in a country where working with people one knows and trusts is of primary importance.

The overwhelming majority of women work on farms or their home-based family businesses. They are the backbone of a number of industries in Punjab, and their particular needlework skills are utilized in many workshops. Most businesses headed by women operate from home, and financial matters may be taken care of by male family members. Women entrepreneurs here opt for traditional businesses such as beauty parlors, bakeries, and boutiques, but the largest number are employed in the garment and handicrafts sectors. Urban women are better informed than those operating in rural areas. However, economic necessity is forcing more and more women, both urban and rural, to engage in some sort of employment or family business without relieving them of their traditional roles.

"THROUGH PROPER CHANNEL"

Pakistanis love to show their importance in the workplace, and especially in an office. Big companies have layers of management, administrative staff, personal assistants, and secretaries, who sometimes try to wield power by not allowing you to speak to their boss directly. The effect of this formal obstructionism is commonly known as going "through proper channel," a phrase formerly used in bureaucratic correspondence, when a clerk would see a file, write a note on it, then pass it on to a head clerk who, adding his own notes, would pass it on a manager. A clerk could hold on to a file for months if not suitably bribed.

If you send an e-mail to the chairman of a company, the chances are that a secretary will reply. Other "gatekeepers," such as junior managers or clerks, mostly out of curiosity and self-importance, may pretend it is necessary for them to obtain all kinds of details from you. The best way to deal with them is to ask their name and rank on the phone in the very first conversation. It is frustrating to speak to a new person on the phone and have to give the information all over again.

ARRANGING A MEETING

Normally the heads of small companies are easily contactable directly, and are happy to talk with potential business partners themselves. A good tip when setting up a meeting is to write in the first instence to the head of the company and ask for the name of a person to talk to. Engage a local intermediary before your approach to help work through the language or any other cultural barriers.

If possible, schedule meetings at least a month in advance, in writing. You can telephone to set a date and time, but always follow up in writing to avoid confusion. More modern companies use e-mail, but letters are also used. If at all possible, try not to schedule meetings during Ramadan. The working day is shortened, and since Muslims fast, they would not be able to offer you tea, which is a sign of hospitality.

Since people want to know whom they will be meeting, provide details ahead of time, again in writing, of the titles, positions, and responsibilities of those attending. Showing status is important, as people will take you more seriously. Send a reminder, by telephone, text message, or e-mail, two or three days before the day of the meeting. Be prepared, however, for meetings to be canceled or postponed at short notice.

Choose your hotel and transportation with care. Use the services of others, such as a porter, to avoid being viewed as a low-ranking intermediary.

MEETINGS

It is essential to arrive on time for a business meeting, as both international and local professionals are expected to be punctual. If you have to wait, which can happen, a display of anger will not go over well and will reflect poorly on you. Greet all your counterparts, starting with the person who has the highest professional rank. After the introductions, offer your business card to everyone present. It is not necessary to have it translated into Urdu, but it should show any doctorates, higher degrees, and professional honors, as these denote status. Make sure that it clearly states your professional title, especially if you have the seniority to make decisions. Present your card with your right hand, with the print facing the recipient. Similarly, accept other people's cards using only the right hand. Smile, and make brief eye contact if you are meeting the person for the first time; frequent eye contact is considered impolite. As a polite gesture, study the card for a few seconds before tucking it away. Not reading someone's card can be insulting.

According to Pakistani etiquette it is appropriate for the client, or the person who will be doing most of the purchasing, to start and end the meeting. Meetings generally start with some small talk, for no more than about ten minutes, which may include inquiries about your health, family, and so on. Humor has no place in this setting, and the meeting may be rather formal and reserved. It is not uncommon to have additional observers sitting in. The primary purpose of this first meeting is to become acquainted and build relationships. Little else may happen, and you may actually not get to talk about business at all while the relationship is still being developed. It is unrealistic to expect initial meetings to lead straight to decisions.

In general, Pakistanis have an open-door policy, even when they are in a meeting. This means there may be frequent interruptions. Tea is essential for a meeting, and acts as an icebreaker before you start discussing serious business. Don't be surprised if your hosts break off for prayers or meals without reaching the end of negotiations. In that case, you can ask when the group next convenes, or schedule another meeting to continue.

PRESENTATIONS

Pakistani business meetings are usually a one-man show, where the boss or head of the group will do all the talking and the rest will listen and nod in assent. When making a presentation, decide whether you want to be interrupted for questions or will take them later. Don't be surprised if your invitation to ask questions meets with dead silence, however. That doesn't mean approval or consent. Some people are shy, and simply don't ask questions in a group, and it is common for someone to come up with questions later, at lunch, or even call you on the telephone to clarify a point. On the other hand, Pakistanis in the private sector, who are accustomed to working with international companies, often challenge speakers and ask difficult questions.

PowerPoint presentations are common, and you can check beforehand on the availability of a large screen or other equipment. Presentation materials should be simple, with good, easy-to-understand visuals. Use colorful diagrams and pictures wherever feasible, keep it brief, and avoid complicated terminology or expressions. Samples, models, and demonstrations are all helpful. To sell an idea or a concept, explain it with examples of previous work. Handouts can be used if they have diagrams, but written papers are not always read.

DECISION MAKING

Pakistanis often take a very long time to reach a final decision, so it is important to be patient. Information is rarely shared freely, since privileged information is thought to create a bargaining advantage. If you should change negotiators, the negotiations will have to start over again, as relationships are with the person rather than the company they represent. Some government departments are extremely bureaucratic, and most decisions require several layers of approval. Pakistanis are nonconfrontational, and will seldom say "No" overtly, so be aware of nonverbal clues.

Pakistani companies are hierarchical. Decisions are reached slowly and are usually made by the highest-ranking person. Always show deference to the senior person in the group, who may be the key decision maker. Sometimes the leader of the group may not have the power to make the final decision, and it is important to establish who does. Be prepared to flatter and be flattered, as this is a tool to get goodwill and sometimes a sign of appreciation.

It is not customary to present a Pakistani businessperson with a gift at the first meeting, but it is polite to take your host a small gift if invited to his house for a meal. Building lasting and trusting personal relationships is very important to most Pakistanis, who expect to establish strong bonds with a business partner prior to closing a deal.

NEGOTIATIONS

Pakistani businesspeople are highly skilled negotiators. They are quite diplomatic, and use indirect communication with a lot of hyperbole and similes—for example, "We produce the strongest steel in the world," or "Our product is as good as the Japanese." A seemingly straightforward question does not always receive a clear answer. Asking closed questions, such as "Can you deliver by June?" as well as open questions, like "How will you do it?" will help you to get the required information.

Pakistanis prefer to converse in a noncontroversial manner, so they will say, "I will try" rather than admit that they cannot or will not be able to do something. Therefore, it is important to ask questions in several ways so you can be certain of the answer. Silence is often used to communicate reluctance to commit to a project, and quite often means a "no." So you, too, can use it in the same way if you want to end negotiations.

Sometimes, your counterparts may talk among themselves, switching to their own language and showing emotions, and a discussion may become heated. It is imperative that you remain calm and do not expect that everything will be translated for you. If you are anxious to know what has been said, ask your host politely to interpret so that you have a full picture of the situation.

Pakistanis are used to pursuing multiple goals in parallel. When negotiating, they often take a holistic approach and may jump back and forth between topics rather than addressing them in a sequential order. Negotiators from Western cultures may find this style confusing, irritating, and even annoying. Make sure you keep track of the bargaining progress at all times, and repeatedly emphasize those areas where agreement already exists.

If your counterparts appear to be stalling, assess carefully what this means—are they evaluating the alternatives, or are they are not interested in doing business with you? It could be a tactic to create time pressure in order to obtain concessions. People from fast-paced cultures tend to underestimate how much time negotiations take, and often make the mistake of trying to speed things up.

Don't use high-pressure tactics, as they can be counterproductive. Being harsh or overly persuasive is considered bad form, and if you are hoping for an early deadline for concluding the negotiations, be sure to allow sufficient time to your partners. Be prepared to make several trips if this is necessary to achieve your objectives.

Pakistanis will bargain when negotiating, and you will be expected to do the same. Pricing is usually a more central consideration than services or support backup.  Leave yourself a lot of room for concessions at different stages. It is not advisable to make significant concessions early, since your counterparts will expect further compromises while the bargaining continues. You can use this approach to your advantage, for instance by offering further concessions on condition that the other side gives way on other points that have already been agreed to.

Deceiving techniques are frequently used. These include telling lies and sending fake messages, pretending to be uninterested in the whole deal, or in single concessions, misrepresenting an item's value, or making false demands. Do not take such tactics personally. Verify the information given by the local side through other channels. Similarly,

Pakistanis will treat the information provided by you with caution. They may claim limited authority, stating that they have to ask for their manager's approval. This could be a tactic or the truth.

Pakistani negotiators may use pressure techniques that include making final offers more than once. Do not use tactics such as applying time pressure or making time-limited offers, since they could view these as signs that you are not willing to build a long-term relationship, and may choose to terminate the negotiation. Periods of silence are frequent, and usually reflect a natural inclination rather than the intentional use of a negotiation technique.

You can use threats and warnings, but with caution, as they may affect the relationship adversely if employed too aggressively. As in most strongly relationship-oriented cultures, Pakistani negotiators may sometimes use emotional techniques, such as grimacing, attempting to make you feel guilty, appealing to personal relationships, or hinting that they have been approached by other interested parties, but that they trust you more, and so on. Be cautious about using any of these tactics yourself. Causing the other side to lose face could damage your negotiating position. Defensive tactics may be used, such as blocking or changing the subject, asking probing questions, or implying that previously made promises may be withdrawn. A promise of exclusivity shows you mean what you say.

CONTRACTS

All contracts are written in English, sometimes in old-fashioned, colonial-era language, though modern contracts are used by IT businesses.

Capturing and exchanging written understandings after meetings and at key stages of a negotiation is useful, since oral statements are not always dependable, but don't mistake interim commitments for the final agreement. Any part of an agreement may still change significantly before both parties sign the contract.

Although most businesspeople in Pakistan understand the role of contracts well, they may view them only as general guides for conducting business, expecting that both parties will be willing to change the terms if there is a change of conditions. Written contracts tend to be lengthy, spelling out detailed terms and conditions for the core agreement as well as for many eventualities. Multiple signatures may be required on the Pakistani side. Nevertheless, writing up and signing the contract is a formality. Pakistanis believe that the primary strength of an agreement lies in the partners' commitment rather than in the written word.

As we have seen, the most frustrating factor for Pakistani companies is the frequency of power outages and rolling blackouts, which affect the delivery of goods. However, although these factors may be a genuine cause of delays, they can sometimes become an excuse for noncompliance. Therefore, it is important to specify a realistic final delivery date in your contract. You should iron out any ambiguous clauses in the contract if in doubt. Although your legal rights may not always be enforceable, it is strongly advisable to consult a local legal expert before signing a contract. However, don't bring your lawyer to the negotiation table, since this may be taken as a sign that you do not trust your counterparts.

A signed contract may not always be honored. Business partners usually expect the other side to remain flexible if conditions change, which may include agreeing to modify the contract's terms.

DISPUTES

Contract enforcement presents a major challenge to Pakistan's business environment. The courts are subject to cumbersome administrative and regulatory requirements, with the result that a dispute is often settled informally rather than in court. Pakistanis try to avoid conflict, and will try to resolve differences through negotiation rather than litigation, which takes a long time and is very expensive.

Should a dispute arise at any point in the fulfillment of a contract, you might be able to reach resolution by leveraging your personal relationships and emphasizing long-term benefits. Refrain from using logical reasoning or becoming argumentative, since this would only make matters worse. Patience and creativity will pay dividends. In extreme situations, use a mediator, ideally the party who initially introduced you.

CORRUPTION

Many expressions and euphemisms are used for small bribery, in different contexts and according to the regional languages. The concept of money for *chai-pani* (tea and water), *shukrana* (thanksgiving), *labbjabb* (give and take), and *mithaee* (sweets) is well understood, and *muthhi garam karo* means "to warm someone's fist." If you notice a porter jumping to the front of a line at an airport, the passenger may have given him a tip for *chai*, on top of the official rate, for getting him or her through more quickly.

Public services have lengthy bureaucratic procedures that force people to pay gatekeepers, receptionists, or clerks to speed up their job. However, people may view these minor payments as rewards rather than bribes. Also, there is a fine line between giving gifts and making bribes. What you may consider a bribe, a Pakistani may see as a gift, and hinting that you view it differently could be a grave insult to his honor. It may help if you introduce and explain your company's policies on receiving gifts early on, but be careful not to moralize or appear to imply that local customs are unethical.

That said, corruption, both petty and grand, is widespread, systematic, and entrenched at all levels of society, especially in government departments. In 2011, Pakistan ranked thirty-fourth on the Transparency International global list of the most corrupt countries in the world. Important business publications, such as the World Economic Forum's *Global Competitiveness Report* (2007–08), says that corruption is the third-greatest problem for companies doing business in Pakistan. Bribery is prevalent in law enforcement, procurement, and the provision of public services, where poorly paid employees have *ooper ki amdani* (Urdu, "income from the top," meaning they top up their salaries). The judiciary is not seen as independent, and is thought to be shielding corrupt political practices from prosecution. Much of the allocation for infrastructure development and a significant portion of the funds for public works are lost due to bribery and related illegal and unethical activities, such as a government official or his/her business partner receiving money in exchange for awarding a contract, job, promotion, or approving invoices for payment. Family ties are very important in the business environment, and often personal favors, rather than money, are granted to get a job done.

Pakistan's location next to Afghanistan, the world's largest producer of opium, makes it vulnerable to drug trafficking. Around 44 percent of the heroin produced in Afghanistan passes through Pakistan; its destination value was estimated at approximately US$27 billion in 2011. The illegal economy and trade in the tribal areas stem from poor socio-economic conditions. Despite a lot of discussion about the problem in development forums, drug trafficking continues unabated.

FOREIGN BUSINESSWOMEN

Pakistanis are generally respectful to women, but business is still a male-dominated field and it is harder for women to make a mark. If you are a visiting businesswoman, emphasize your company's importance and your role in it. A personal introduction, or at least a letter of support from a senior executive within your company, may also help. If you are the head of your company, it is advisable to take a male colleague as an assistant along for the trip. You should exercise caution and act professionally in both business and social situations. Displaying confidence and assertiveness can be counterproductive, and being overly bold and aggressive can create major issues. Loud, boisterous behavior is perceived as a lack of self-control.

Female business travelers need to dress in accordance with local customs, which means modestly. You don't have to wear local dress. Some women have found that if they wear a smart long skirt and a full-sleeved shirt they are regarded as more businesslike. Avoid wearing heavy makeup, strong perfume, and loads of jewelry, which will give the impression of a lack of seriousness.

COLLEAGUES

As we have seen, Pakistanis like to do business with people they know and trust. Consequently, family members and friends are often hired to work in the same company. This has created a culture of obliging and covering up the faults of each other. The term "teamwork" in Pakistan means depending on each other for day-to-day tasks and covering for colleagues when they are absent. Individual performance and working independently are avoided, so that the responsibility for failure is shared. Pakistani bosses can be very paternal and protective of their colleagues, and at times employee accountability is impossible.

Managers are seen as the most powerful people in the office, who can make or break the careers of employees. Family background and contacts are as important for a manager as educational qualifications. They are used to giving and receiving orders, therefore working with teams where consensus is necessary is a challenge for them.

Older people and those in senior positions are deferred to and treated with dignity and respect. Women tend to occupy subordinate roles; they generally have little exposure to business life and lack peer support. However, more women can be seen in the workplace than a few years ago.

Pakistani workers appreciate and sometimes expect recognition or rewards for their hard work. People are polite, and are not very likely to complain about their superiors or their management style, but employees' performances improve if they are happy with their superior.

MANAGING DISAGREEMENT

Each person has a distinct role within a Pakistani organization, and maintaining that role helps to keep order. Managers are supposed to observe a degree of formality at all times, in keeping with their status. You may find middle managers autocratic in their style of dealing with workers, but that is considered normal. Honor and reputation play an important part, and it is necessary to respond to ideas that are raised in a gentle, nonconfrontational manner, protecting the reputation of those bringing up ideas, so that no one is shamed.

Workers in Pakistan are under immense pressure physically, with electricity breakdowns, deprivation of sleep due to hot weather, and mosquitoes, to name just a few examples. However, there is commitment to achieving deadlines, and when under pressure people do deliver on time. A boss is seen as a paternalistic figure, and is expected to assist subordinates with their personal problems. To ensure successful cross-cultural management, you will need to bear in mind the importance of people in the office maintaining the proper behavior relative to their position. The environment in offices is still not favorable for women, and harassment in one form or another commonly takes place without comment.

Most people do not criticize others to their face, and try to avoid confrontation. High performers have the most difficult position in a team, and if they are rewarded, jealousy might be a cause of conflict and grievance. Few people would question or criticize a decision in a meeting, even if they are not happy with it. Therefore it is best to get feedback individually if possible before implementation. Pakistanis are scared of losing face, and it is very hard for them to apologize after a mistake has been made. In some Pakistani cultures, an apology means weakness. Similarly, when a person does apologize, the recipient may accept it superficially but retain hard feelings for a long time.

chapter nine

COMMUNICATING

LANGUAGE
There are more than seventy known languages
spoken throughout Pakistan, which all belong to the
Indo-Aryan family. Those that are written use Arabic
script. The four provinces have large numbers of
Punjabi, Pashto, Sindhi, Balochi, Siraiki, and Hindko
speakers. Urdu is the national language, but it is not
the mother tongue of the majority of the population.
However, it is the main language of communication
between the various peoples of Pakistan. Most
Pakistanis are bilingual, and a large majority speak or
understand more than two languages. Some people
can switch comfortably from one language
to another, and there is no shortage of
different dialects and accents in each
regional language. Pakistani children
speak their mother tongue till school age;
they learn to read Arabic through Quranic
studies, and are taught in Urdu at school.
English is learned at secondary school, and is
the medium of instruction at university.

English is the official language and is used in all
government documents, military communications,
street and shop signs, business contracts, colleges,
and universities. Almost all conversations of city
dwellers, in whatever language, have a significant

English component. Therefore, as a general rule, you can get away with speaking English in the urban areas of Pakistan.

Sahibs, Sirs, and Others

Pakistani names often include a title that denotes a person's ethnic group, class, tribe, occupation, or other status indicator. They may also include two names that have a specific meaning when used together, and the meaning is lost if the names are separated (see below). It is best to ask a person how they wish to be addressed. In general, this is not a culture where first names are commonly used, except among close friends. In public places the title of "Sahib" is used with men's names, and in the different regional accents it is pronounced in different ways, such as *sahib* in Urdu, *saab jee* in Punjab, and *saib* in Balochi and Pashto. It is equivalent to Mr., but is used either after a first name, as in Mushtaq Sahib, or after a surname, like Khan Sahib. The title of Sahib is also used for a boss or another person with authority.

For women the title of "Sahiba" is also used in formal and business conversations, as in Nasreen Sahiba. "Miss" is used to address or refer to female teachers, and "Sister" for female nurses. Both these titles are also used to address or refer to women colleagues or subordinates. "Madam" is used to address and refer to women in positions of authority, usually a superior.

You don't need to be knighted to obtain the title of "Sir" in Pakistan, but you need to be an army officer or a male teacher at university or college level. "Sir" is also used to address a male superior, often combined with their name or used as a proper noun. Junior members of the armed forces use "Sir" with their officers' names when referring to them— for example, Khalid Siddiqui will be called either "Sir Khalid" or "Sir Siddiqui." Pakistanis use the English title "Mr." when speaking to a foreigner, even with his first name, as in Mr. Andrew, or Mr. John, unless asked not to do so. You can do this too, and address Akhlaq Khan as Mr. Khan or Mr. Akhlaq.

Some names are compounds of two words—for example, Shahidullah, shortened to Shahid (but don't mistake the second part of the name, "Ullah," for a surname). Similarly, Abdulsamad becomes "Samad," and "Abdul" will not be used as a first name.

There are certain titles of respect that become part of the name, similar to Doctor or Professor, or to a rank of the army such as Colonel, Major, and so on. Here are a few, and you can use "Sahib" after the title:

Sayyed	Sayyed Sahib (Arabic, master)
Pir or Peer	Peer Sahib (holy one)
Haji	Haji Sahib (one who went to Mecca for Hajj)
Doctor	Doctor Sahib

"Master Sahib," contracted to "Ma'Sahib" is used frequently to refer to a master tailor. The Arabic title "Ustad" (teacher) is frequently used in everyday language for a bus driver, or a craftsman. This word is also used for a person who is smart or clever.

Pakistani English

All educated Pakistanis can communicate in English, and sometimes mix it heavily with their own languages or Urdu. The affluent will use the words "sorry" or "thank you" even if they are talking among themselves in their own language. If a mother wants her child to apologize, she will say, "Sorry *karro*" (literally, "do sorry"), or a young man will greet his friends with, "*Mera* wait *karro*" (wait for me).

In all Pakistani languages polite words equivalent to please, pardon me, and thank you do exist but are not used as commonly as in English. As a result, Pakistanis seem very direct when speaking other languages. For example, they will say, "Give me that paper," without adding "please," which sounds like an abrupt order, rather than a request, to a native English speaker. If someone says, "Come to my house for a meal," it is a genuine invitation, as opposed to "Visit me next time," which is a mere politeness. If you wish to decline politely, you can say, "Next time." If you are being pressed to come, just say "No thank you."

Some phrases, such as "could be," " might be," or "would be," can be misunderstood. If you say, for example, "I might see the minister," it may be wrongly understood as a definite plan to see the minister. If you are not sure that you will be able to see him, rephrase it as, "I am trying to see the minister but have not made an appointment yet."

Ailments and diseases are mentioned in English, for example, "*Mujhe* heart problem *hay*," or "*Mera* cholesterol high *hay*," or even "Bone fracture *hay*."

Greetings and Partings

Almost all Pakistanis greet each other with *Assalamualaikum* (peace be upon you) and reply *Waalaikum assalam* (and upon you peace). Young, upwardly mobile Pakistanis will say "hello," "good morning," and "good-bye" as well. In every region and language there are traditional greetings that you can learn easily from your Pakistani colleagues. Some visitors make the mistake of holding their hands together in the Indian style when greeting a Pakistani, but this gesture is not appropriate. Putting your right hand over your heart is a polite gesture of greeting in some regions.

Members of the same sex often greet each other by shaking hands and/or embracing. Men generally shake hands with each other, and to show warmth sometimes a host will put his left hand on top of the guest's right hand. A woman should not initiate a handshake with a man, but she can with other women. The senior women of the household will embrace the visiting women, in some regions three times—from right to left shoulder, and then again right. Younger women may kiss the right hand of an elderly lady, who in return kisses her on the forehead when she takes her leave. Men will embrace once a relationship has developed, but in some areas it is usual to embrace a guest on the first visit. Sometimes an elderly or religious man will put the palm of his hand on the head of a younger guest as a sign of blessing.

Pakistanis take their time during greetings, and ask about the person's health, family, and business success. They often ask personal questions as a way of getting to know you, and go out of their way to find something to praise. It is also customary for a Pakistani to reply "fine" or "*Alhamdulillah*" (praise to God) when asked about their health, even if they are not well. It is common to say "*Khuda ka shuker hai*" (thank God) as an answer to any inquiry about one's health, family, or business, regardless of the facts. When leaving a gathering it is customary to say "*Khuda hafiz*" (may God protect you) in Urdu, or a valediction in the local language.

MANNERS AND BODY LANGUAGE

The first-time visitor is usually struck by the lack of smiles in Pakistan. Smiling at strangers in public is not common practice, but that does not mean people are unhappy. Direct eye contact is not that important for Pakistanis, and it is considered rude to speak to somebody while gazing into their eyes. Women will usually avoid looking into an unknown man's face, and will lower their eyes when speaking. Avoid prolonged eye contact with the opposite sex, as this can be misunderstood as a sexual advance on your part. Staring, however, is quite common and is not considered rude; it may make you feel uncomfortable.

Pakistanis are generally indirect communicators, and speak in a roundabout fashion. Direct statements are made only to those with whom they have a long-standing personal relationship. Most people are talkative and speak loudly; they will stand close to you while conversing and you may feel as if your personal space has been violated.

Vulgar hand gestures used in Western cultures are understood in Pakistan and should be avoided. Traditionally, the thumbs-up gesture is an offensive insult to Muslims. It is equivalent to showing the middle finger in the Western world. More media-savvy Pakistanis may understand the Western meaning of an upturned thumb, while others may still use the gesture in its traditional sense.

Winking always has sexual connotations, and should be avoided. In some rural areas, pounding your fist into your palm or stroking your beard or mustache signals revenge. Avoid pointing a finger at objects or at a person to whom you wish to speak. To point at or beckon others with the finger is rude and can be construed as a sexual advance.

You'll notice the segregation of men and women in public places, such as airports, hospitals, and railway and bus stations. Seats are offered to women or the elderly, and men not related to a woman will avoid sitting next to her out of respect. If you are introduced to elders or strangers when seated it is customary to get up as sign of respect. The soles of shoes, sandals, or feet are considered unclean, so you shouldn't sit in a way that exposes them to company. This is also the reason for removing shoes when entering the sitting area in a home or in shrines and mosques.

Food is mostly handled with the right hand—for example, when offering a dish, drinking, or giving a glass of water to another person. Left-handed people learn to use their right hand. Don't use a knife to cut *roti or naan*. A small piece is torn from the bread with your right hand to pinch or scoop the food between thumb and fingers. Leaving food is wasteful, but in some regions it is considered gracious and a sign of having had enough. It is for you to balance how much food to leave on the plate to avoid extra offers without being rude. In some areas your host might think you are not eating out of politeness and put more food on your empty plate. If you are faced with this situation, it is perfectly normal to cover your plate with your right hand to show that you don't want more.

Spitting in public is rude. Though you may well see people doing it in the streets they are frowned upon. Also undesirable are breaking wind in public, producing the sound of a fart from your mouth, sitting on the floor with your legs apart, and showing physical affection to the opposite sex in public.

Pakistanis are liberal with their hand gestures and facial expressions during conversation, and many of these are universal. A scowl, grimace, or frown means the same thing in Pakistan as in the rest of the world. Unlike the Indians, Pakistanis nod their heads up and down for "yes" and left to right for "no."

HUMOR

Facial expressions, jokes, and parody are the favorite kinds of Pakistani humor. Traditionally, at weddings or get-togethers in rural areas, locally recognized comics would entertain the community with farcical dialogues and slapstick comedy. They are still widely popular in Punjab, patronized by the elite, who invite them to perform at private parties. They are known as *bhand* (in some places, *mirasi*), and are so bold in their jokes that even the most powerful figures in the community are not spared, but they are respected, and nobody takes offense. Professional parodists, known as *naqqal*, are expert in mimicry or caricature. In rural areas when the sun goes down impromptu comedians crack jokes to local audiences.

Pakistani screen comedians are famous in the areas where people have access to film and television; their humor is more sophisticated, sometimes with a political angle to it. Mr. Bean (Rowan Atkinson) is a popular movie character, along with old-time favorites such as Charlie Chaplin.

Popular frustration with military rule, political instability, and social injustice often comes out in the form of sarcastic jokes about taboo subjects. Most Pakistanis enjoy sharing jokes with others for a good laugh. Two out of three people have a cell phone, and the cost of sending an SMS is among the lowest in the world, which has given the masses freedom to text political jokes immediately after an important event.

This is perhaps the most effective means of letting off steam, and a way of expressing solidarity. It seems that nothing is sacred in an SMS joke, which is read aloud for the group to enjoy.

You may notice that people are laughing at something funny, but will become serious if you add another funny comment. This can sometimes be taken as an insult, and can backfire. The best thing in such situation is to smile politely.

A favorite phrase is "This is Pakistan," used in everyday conversation when things get out of control. In front of a foreigner, though, people may be more careful, and self-deprecation is avoided.

Sometimes a catchphrase is coined that makes people smile. For example, "Direct *havaldar*" means a person appointed to a post without competition or fair selection, or who is promoted out of turn or given undeserved authority—a *havaldar* was equivalent to a sergeant in the British Indian Army.

THE MEDIA

The first Pakistani newspapers and magazines were founded in the nineteenth century and were the main source of information for the educated. Radio, and later television, was owned by the government, and during the political upheavals of the last two decades of the twentieth century editorial policy was dictated by the establishment or the party in power. In 2001 the military regime, under immense internal and international pressure, opened up the electronic media market to local and foreign investors. The resultant growth of privately owned TV and radio channels has exposed the Pakistani public to ninety national and twenty-eight foreign TV channels.

There are more than a hundred licensed FM radio stations and countless pirate FM stations, run by religious groups and individuals in troubled areas of the country, especially in the tribal areas.

In 2002, the government established an electronic media regulatory body called PEMRA (Pakistan Electronic Media Regulatory Authority), with the mandate to issue licenses to private firms to operate in the Pakistani media market. This authority is also responsible for regulating electronic media content, distribution, and monitoring; hence it can ban or fine any channel or company for not following the terms and criteria laid down by the government.

In today's environment, TV channels inflame and polarize public debate. The private channels are competing for viewers, and some anchors and moderators have turned them into real-time media circuses, which can sometimes be irresponsible and reckless. Serious talk programs have become entertainment shows, where all the participants speak at the same time and the anchor either seems helpless or deliberately encourages confrontation.

Newspapers and Magazines

The last decade has seen a marked decline in the number of daily newspapers and magazines, which have been losing business and readership to growing television exposure. About a hundred daily papers are published in Pakistan, mostly in Urdu, followed by English. While young people are increasingly getting their information from the Internet and from the social media, most educated people still read newspapers, and some of Pakistan's English-language dailies have high-quality content and deal with national and international issues.

Press freedom in Pakistan is precarious. It is limited by the official censorship that restricts critical reporting and by the high level of violence against journalists. Although some journalists practice self-censorship, a wide range of privately owned daily and weekly newspapers and magazines do provide critical coverage of national affairs. Topics that frequently attract the government's attention are the armed forces, the judiciary, and religion, but the English-language newspapers usually get away with making a point, as they are not widely read in the country.

Some of the big newspapers are privately owned, and there are a few news groups that publish English and Urdu dailies alongside weekly or monthly magazines. For example, the Jang group publishes daily broadsheets and tabloid weekly magazines in both languages. The Dawn group publishes its flagship broadsheet, *Dawn*, and a monthly magazine, *Herald*, both in English. The Nawai Waqt group has an Urdu daily of the same name and a children's Urdu magazine, *Phool*. All these publications are based in Karachi and Lahore, with offices in other provinces. Pakistan's first English-language business newspaper is the *Business Recorder*, published in Karachi.

The only English-language newspaper based in Peshawar is the *Frontier Post*, which is distributed throughout Pakistan and Afghanistan. A daily Urdu newspaper, *Mashriq*, and the Pashto-language *Wahdat* are also published in Peshawar. The only Balochi newspaper, *Nawai Watan*, is published and distributed in Quetta, and there are a number of monthly and weekly magazines in other languages published and circulated locally. The main political parties of Pakistan have their own magazines in the local and national languages.

TELEPHONE AND INTERNET

Approximately 90 percent of Pakistanis live within
areas that have cell phone coverage, and most people
have access to a cell phone. With 118 million mobile
subscribers in 2012, Pakistan has the highest mobile
penetration rate in the South Asian region. The
government, as the main facilitator, enabler, and
promoter of the IT sector, has evolved a
national policy to nurture the industry. The
private sector is being brought into the
mainstream as the main driver for growth.
Internet access can be obtained easily on
notebook computers with the help of GPRS-
enabled mobile connections, supported by
almost all of the five mobile operators—
Mobilink, Telenor, Zong, Ufone, and Warid.
The national telecommunications company, PTCL,
offers the latest devices for fast Internet connection.
Nokia cited Pakistan as having the third-highest SMS
traffic in the world in 2010. You will see young men
and women rapidly sending texts on their cell phones
and talking to others at the same time.

Cyber cafés can be found on virtually every street
corner of the big cities, and the rates are as low as
Rs.15–20 (around 15-20 US cents) per hour. Most of
the cafés have decent high-speed Internet connection,
but electricity breakdowns may cause delays, so don't
be too impatient. There are several Wi-Fi hot spots in
Pakistan, in hotels, malls, cafés, and restaurants.

For a quick landline telephone call, PCOs (Public
Call Offices), situated in corner shops, are best. They
can be found all over the country in nearly 50 percent
of the general stores, and are indicated by a sign.
There is usually someone who operates the phone
and fax and will dial the number for you. You need to

ask the rate for a call and fees will be charged according to the time spent. Have some cash in Pakistani money ready, and normally you will pay when you have finished your call or sending your fax.

MAIL

The postal service started life in the city of Lahore in 1898. There were hundreds of post offices throughout the country, providing services such as delivering parcels and letters, sending and receiving telegrams, pensions, money transfers, and issuing licenses.

The state postal service is called Pakistan Post. General Post Offices (GPO) control all the small post offices in a province, train staff, and provide postage, parcel, and financial services. These services are cheaper than those offered by private companies but may not be reliable. With the growth of new technology and privatization, the services have declined in recent years, and a number have been transferred to local banks. For further information, see the Web site (http://www.pakpost.gov.pk).

For a more reliable service, there are international courier companies such as FedEx, TCS, and Leopard, which have offices in the big cities, but are expensive.

CONCLUSION

Pakistan is besieged by bad news. The world media focus on extremism, corruption, and political crises. All these problems notwithstanding, the true picture is infinitely more complex and rewarding. Pakistan's rich traditions reflect a long history of migrations. A myriad local festivals and celebrations and a vibrant cultural life go unremarked.

Strong family ties, hospitality, and respect for human feelings are at the core of this society. That Pakistan has stayed on its feet despite a decade of misfortune in the twenty-first century is mainly due to its workforce and to its well-established system of governance. Despite the turmoil, there is world-class progress and development, from skyscraper complexes to solar power generation fields.

Daily life for Pakistanis is full of difficulties, yet everyone knows how to cope. People quickly find alternatives to the shortage of fuel or electricity and carry on as normal: a housewife will find ways to prepare a meal for the family using charcoal in her modern kitchen, or a dish that does not require cooking. Recycle and reuse is the norm, and it is this characteristic adaptability that holds communities together. There is a Pashto proverb that sums up the spirit of the nation: "Although my house has been burned, its walls, made of bricks baked in the sun, have been strengthened by baking in fire."

You can see the generosity of the people in the many charities in the country, which work with remarkable resilience. Ordinary Pakistanis have donated millions to the Edhi Foundation, a welfare trust that had humble beginnings in Karachi in 1951, and which today has 1,800 ambulances—the largest fleet in the world.

Pakistan recently granted "Most Favored Nation" status to its old enemy, India, as a trading partner—a significant and hopeful sign of a balanced and functioning democracy. Flexible and pragmatic, the Pakistanis have a record of recovery from setbacks. Earn their trust, and you will discover the friendship of an extraordinarily talented, tough, passionate, and loyal people.

Appendix

SOME EVERYDAY PAKISTANI EXPRESSIONS

His/her meter has turned high	He/she has had a sudden outburst of anger
Where are you put up?	Where are you staying?
How do you pass time?	What are your hobbies?
Shirtings and suitings	This shop specializes in men's formal and business wear
No lift	No attention, as in "I tried to make an appointment, but Mr. Khan gave me no lift"
Same to same	Exactly the same
Gentry	Denotes social class, with a prefix of good, bad, or high
Double roti	Bread
Shopper	Plastic carrier bag
Numbers	Marks. "How many numbers?" means "How many marks?" (in an exam)
Co-brother	Two (otherwise unrelated) men married to two sisters
Co-sister	Two (otherwise unrelated) women married to two brothers
Rubber	Eraser
Pent	Trousers
Pindrop silence	Extreme silence
Hill station	Mountain resort
Cent per cent	100 percent
Loose motion	Diarrhea
Expire	To die
Dicky/dickey/digy	The trunk or boot of a car
With sugar	Diabetic
Allopathy treatment	Conventional medicine
Too much	Very much

SOME URDU WORDS AND THEIR MEANINGS

Lakh, or *lac*	One hundred thousand
Crore	Ten million
Arrab	One billion
One *kharrab*	One hundred billion
Accha	Good/OK/really
Shukria	Thank you
Theek hai	It's right/fine
Zaroor	Definitely
Yaar	My friend
Zabardast	Fantastic

Further Reading

Albinia, Alice. *Empires of the Indus: The Story of a River.* London: John Murray, 2008.

Singh, Sarina, et al. *Pakistan and the Karakoram Highway.* Victoria, Australia: Lonely Planet, 2008.

Dani, Ahmad Hsan. *History of Northern Areas of Pakistan.* Lahore: Sang-i-Meel Publications, 2001.

Hashmi, Salima, et al. *Hanging Fire: Contemporary Art from Pakistan.* New York: Asia Society, 2009.

Leiven, Anatol. *Pakistan: A Hard Country.* London: Allen Lane, 2011.

Malik, Iftikhar. *Culture and Customs of Pakistan.* Culture and Customs of Asia. Westport, CT: Greenwood Press, 2005.

Mortenson, Greg, and David Oliver Relin. *Three Cups of Tea: One Man's Mission to Promote Peace … One School at a Time.* London: Penguin Books, 2006.

culture smart! pakistan

Index

9/11 attacks (September 11, 2001) 30, 82
Abdali, Ahmad Shah 23
accommodation 126–27
address, forms of 88, 151–52
Afghanistan 10, 12, 14, 23, 27, 28, 30, 116, 118, 119, 129, 146
air travel 116–17, 119
Al-Qaeda 30
alcohol 86, 103, 106
Alexander of Macedonia 20–21
All-India Muslim League 24
Ambhi, King 20
art 8, 13, 56, 63, 108
Ashoka 20
Ashura 41, 45–46
astrologers (*najumis*) 73
Awami National Party (ANP) 32
Azad Jammu and Kashmir 10, 26–27, 51

Babur 22
Baha'i faith 41
Bakhsh, Allah 108
Balochistan 10, 14, 15, 18, 25, 29–30, 39, 69, 97–98, 104, 110
festivals 61–62
Bangladesh 12, 29
Bhitai, Shah Abdul Latif 63
Bhutto, Benazir 31, 32, 33
Bhutto, Zulfikar Ali 29, 30, 32, 34
birth 69–70
birthdays 70
body language, manners and 155–57
Bolan Pass 26, 118–19
borders 117–19
Buddhism, Buddhists 20, 21, 57, 72
bureaucracy 37, 52–53
burqa 47
buses 118, 120, 121–23
business cards 136–37
business culture 133–34

calendars 57, 58
call to prayer (*azan*) 42
caste system (*zat*) 41

censorship 110, 160
Chambers of Commerce and Industry 132
character 9, 163
charities 163
children 36, 39, 95–97
China 10, 14, 15, 118
Chota-Lahure 22
Christians 11, 17, 41, 57
Chughtai, Abdul Rahman 108
cinema 110
circumcision 70
climate 10, 16, 114–15
colleagues 147–48
contracts 142–44
conversation, making 79–80
corruption 8, 33, 40, 52–53, 144–46, 162
cricket 8–9, 13, 106
cultural activities 108–10
currency 11, 114, 133

Dahir, Raja 22
dance 60–67, 100, 110
dating 87, 98
decision making 139
disagreement, managing 148–49
disputes 144
divorce 42, 48
dowry 69
drama 109
dress 44, 46–47, 56, 84, 114, 131, 147
drinks 105–6, 127
driving 124–25
drug trafficking 146
Durand Line 26, 27–28, 30
Durand, Mortimer 27

earthquakes 8, 15
East Bengal 25
East India Company 23
East Pakistan 26, 28, 29
eating out 101–2
economy 34–35
education 96–97
attitudes to 54–55
further 97–98
and women 55
Eid-ul-Adha 59
Eid-ul-Fitr 46, 58–59
electricity 11, 89, 115,

127, 128, 148, 161
emergency numbers 131
entrepreneurs 134
ethnic groups 10, 17, 40–41
evil eye (*nazar*) 74–75
extended families 38, 48, 49, 59, 69, 70, 71, 93–94, 99, 100
eye contact 155

Faisalabad 10, 14, 111–12, 119
family 9, 36, 38–39, 147, 163
family living 91–93
visits 70–71
FATA (Federally Administered Tribal Areas) 10, 28, 30–31
festivals 162
religious 56, 57, 58–60
seasonal 56, 60–66
feudal system 39–40
Five Pillars of Islam 41–42
folklore and superstition 72–77
food 101–5
hygiene 128
manners 156
foreigners, attitudes to 81–82
friendship 78–79
funerals 71–72

Gandhara kingdom 12, 19, 20, 20–21
geography 14–16
gestures 155, 156
gifts 49, 59, 85–86
business 139
Gilgit-Baltistan 10
Gillani, Syed Yusuf Raza 33
globalization 50
government 10, 33–34
greetings 70, 79, 136, 153–54
guesthouses 127

hajj (pilgrimage) 42, 59, 69
halal 103
handshakes 70, 83, 154
Harappa 18
health 127–29

henna 59, 67–68
hierarchy 36, 135, 139
hijab 47, 55
Hindus 11, 17, 24, 25,
  26, 41, 57, 72
history 17–26
  prehistory 17–18
  the Indus 18–19
  the Aryans 19
  the Persians 19–20
  the Bactrian Greeks
    20–21
  the Huns 21–22
  the Afghans 22–23
  the Arabs 22
  the British Raj 23–24
  independence 24–26
holidays, public 57–58
homosexuality 50
honor 9, 37, 47–48, 148
hospitality 9, 37, 48–49,
  82, 84, 85
hotels 126–27, 128
housing 88–91
hugs 50, 70, 83, 95
humor 157–58
Hussain, Imam 45, 60
Hyderabad 10, 26

imams 43
Independence Day 57
India 10, 12, 14, 22–29,
  72, 116, 163
Indo-Aryans 10, 17
Indus civilization 8, 12,
  18–19
Indus River 8, 12, 15, 18,
  20, 28
inflation 35
inheritance 42
International Monetary
  Fund 35
Internet 81, 87, 98–99,
  159, 161
  domain 11
invitations home 82–85
Iqbal, Muhammad
  57–58
Iran 10, 14, 118
Islam 11, 41–47, 54
Islamabad 10, 65–66,
  104, 116, 119, 120,
  123, 124
Islamic year 58–60
Ismaili Muslims 41
Israel 115–16

Jamaat-e-Islami 32
Jamiat-ul-Ulema-Islam
  32
jehad (holy war) 30

Jews 115–16
Jinnah, Muhammad Ali
  24, 25
  anniversary of 57
  birthday of 57
jinns 75–76
Junagadh 26

K2 mountain 14, 15, 113
kala jadoo (black magic)
  77
Karachi 10, 14, 41, 91,
  116, 119, 124, 126
Karakorum Range 15,
  16
Kashmir 10, 15, 26–27,
  51, 57
Khan, Amir Abdur
  Rahman 27
Khan, General
  Muhammed Ayub 28
Khan, Nusrat Fateh Ali
  109
Khan, General Yahya 29
Kharoshti 20
Khyber Pakhtunkhwa
  (formerly North-
  West Frontier
  Province) 10, 18, 97,
  105, 110
  festivals 64–65
Khyber Pass 14, 18, 26,
  113, 118
kismet 37, 73

Labor Day 57
Lahore 10, 14, 23, 66,
  91, 111, 113, 116,
  119, 120, 124
language 9, 11, 41, 130,
  150–54
  everyday expressions
    164
  Pakistani English
    152–53
Leghari, Farooq 32
literary activities 66–67
losing face 142, 149
love and marriage
  98–99

madrassas (religious
  schools) 45, 54, 96
magazines 158, 159, 160
magic 77
Mahmud, King 22
Makkah (Mecca) 42, 43,
  69
mannat 74
manners and body
  language 155–57

Mansura 22
marriage 39, 41, 42, 48,
  50, 67–69, 98
mashvara (consultation)
  99
Maurya, Chandra
  Gupta, Emperor 20
media 158–60
medical treatment 129
meetings 136–38
  arranging 135–36
Mehergarh, Balochistan
  17–18
melas 60–61, 62, 64
migration 12, 26, 162
Mihirakula, Hunnish
  Emperor 21
Mirza, Iskandar,
  President 28
Mohammad, Prophet
  37, 42, 45, 51, 130
  birthday of 59–60
Mohenjodaro 18, 19,
  112
mosques 43, 44, 59
Mughals 22, 23
Muhajirs 41, 69
Muharram 60
Mukti Bahini 29
Multan 120
Musharraf, General
  Pervez 28, 33
music 13, 60–67, 100,
  109, 110, 122–23
Muslim League 32
Muslims 12–13, 17, 22,
  24, 25, 26, 41–47,
  103, 106, 136
Muttahidda Qaumi
  Movement (MQM)
  32

naseehat (advice-giving)
  99
negotiations 139–42
nepotism 40, 134
newspapers 158, 159–60
North-West Frontier
  Province 25, 27–28
nuclear weapons 8

outside world, attitudes
  to the 50–51

Pakistan Muslim League
  31, 32
Pakistan People's Party
  31, 32, 33
Pakistan Resolution
  24, 57
Pakistani army 8, 30–31

Parsis (Zoroastrians) 17
Partition 12, 26, 27
Pashtuns, Pashtun areas 27, 28, 30, 41, 47, 69, 82, 104, 110, 119
personal questions 80–81, 154
Peshawar 10, 21, 22, 111, 116, 118, 120, 124
photography 82
poetry 66–67, 108, 109
politics 28–33
population 10, 17, 98
pork prohibition 103
Porus, Raja 20
poverty 9, 33, 54
prejudice 50
presentations 138
privacy 94–95
public holidays 57–58
Punjab, Punjabis 10, 13, 16, 18, 23, 26, 32, 47, 69, 102, 103, 104–5, 111, 113
    festivals 62
    purdah 46–47

Qadiyanis 41
Qalandar, Shahbaz 63
Qasim, Mohammad bin 22
Qibla 43
qingqi 123–24
Quetta 10, 116, 118
Quran 44–45, 51, 68, 73, 75, 76, 150

radio 158, 159
rail travel 118, 125–26
Ramadan 42, 46, 53, 58, 59, 136
Rawalpindi 124, 126
refugees 17
religion 11, 17, 36–37, 41–47, 51
remarriage 42
respect 9, 37, 42–45, 51, 70, 78, 82, 84, 85, 146, 148, 156
restaurants 101–2
rickshaws 123–24
rishtaydari 93–94

road transport 120–24
Rohtas fort, Jhelum 113
rolling blackouts 11, 115, 128, 143

sadka (alms) 76
safety 129–31
saints 13, 22, 62–63, 74
sayyeds 37, 45
segregation of men and women 156
shame 47, 48
Sharia law 34
Sharif, Nawaz 31–32, 33
shaving of baby's head, first (aqiqa) 70
Shia Muslims 11, 17, 41, 45–46, 60
shoe removal 84, 156
shopping 92–93
    for pleasure 110–12
shrines 74
Sialkot 14, 21, 112
sightseeing 112–13
Sikhs 17, 23, 26, 41, 57
Silk Road 21, 120
Sindh 10, 13, 16, 18, 22, 25, 39, 47, 102, 104–5
    festivals 62–63
Singh, Ranjit 23
smoking 70
social networks 80
sports and games 100, 106–8
staring 80, 155
status 37, 47, 80, 136, 148, 151
storytelling 66, 109
success, attitudes to 51–52
Sufi saints 13, 22, 62–63
Sunni Muslims 11, 17, 41, 43, 46, 60
superstition, folklore and 72–77

taboos 95
Taleban 30, 31
tanga (horse and carriage) 121
taveez (amulet) 75, 76–77

Taxila 20, 113, 120
taxis 124
telephone 11, 87, 98–99, 114, 131, 157–58, 161–62
    emergency numbers 131
television 11, 100, 110, 158, 159
terrorism 8, 51, 130
theater 109
time-keeping 53–54, 83–84, 136
tolerance 50
toona-totka 77
tourism 114, 125
transvestites 50
the troubles of the tribal areas 30–31

UNESCO World Heritage Sites 112–13

Vedas 19
Victoria, Queen 24
visas 115–16

"wagons" (minibuses) 120
water, drinking 127
wealth 9, 37, 51
weddings 67–69, 93
West Pakistan 26, 28
West Punjab 25
Western influence 50–51
women
    attitudes to foreign women 81–82
    entrepreneurs 134
    in the family 38–39, 92
    foreign businesswomen 146–47
    and purdah 46–47
    travelers 131
work ethic 37, 52–53

Zardari, Asif Ali 33
Zia-ul-Haq, General 30, 31, 110

Acknowledgments

Many thanks to my husband, Adli Hawwari, for his feedback on my writing, to Safdar Hamadani, who provided first-hand information on regional cultures, to Piera Cavenaghi, whose personal experiences offered fresh perspectives, and to many friends who are waiting to read this book.